ALONG THE Testimonies

Gleaned Along the Way

By: Gladys Goldsby Ford
Cover Design By: Kharis Courtney

ALONG THE PILGRIM PATHWAY

Scripture quotations are from the
King James Version of the Bible.
All Greek and Hebrew definitions
are from the Strong's Exhaustive Concordance.

You are welcome to copy portions of this book. However, no portion may be reproduced and sold.

TABLE OF CONTENTS

Page

6	Dedication
7	All That Glitters Isn't Gold
10	And, In the Process of Time
12	As Soon As I See How It Will Go With Me
14	Be Careful Which Ruts You Choose
16	Be It Unto Me According to Thy Word
18	Be Not As the Ostrich
20	Becoming a Rhodes Scholar
23	Between the Promise and the Fulfillment
25	Bird, Your Days Are Numbered
29	Brian Had Been Jerked, Popped, and Slapped
32	But I Didn't Bring Anybody With Me
33	By Little and Little
36	Courthouse Experiences
39	Daddy, You'll Never Be Ashamed of Me Again
43	Dear Abby, I Am a Christian
45	Don't Become an Oxymoron
47	Father, I Need to Tell You Something
49	Frank and Doris Command Money
51	Garments Rolled In Blood
53	Gassed Tomatoes Aren't That Tasty
55	Gee, I hope I Passed the Test
58	Give It a Few Days and It'll All Work Out
60	God of the Ribbons
62	Guess I'll Read It Again
65	Having Loved This Present World
67	He Is Able
69	He Notices How We Give
72	He Warned the Stranger
74	Hello, My Name Is Virginia Lawrence

78	Her Heart Was Bursting
80	Honor the Lord With Thy Substance
83	I Don't Think I Could Add a Thing
85	I Was Just Gonna Smell It, Lord
88	If Brenda Could Talk To You Now
90	If the Lord Be For Us
93	It Was a Man In a Business Suit
96	It's More Than an Ideal Funeral Message
103	It's Not As Pretty As Her Heart
105	Judgment Without Mercy
108	Katie Wants To Trot
110	Knowing Scripture Is Not Enough
112	Lord, I Will Follow Wherever You Tell Me to Go
118	Lord, Pity Us
120	Lord, Teach Us To Savor
122	Lord, Was It Me?
125	Mercy Stood Still
128	My Son, God Will Provide Himself a Lamb
131	Pray and Go On
133	She Hath Done What She Could
136	She Is Not Pushing This
138	She Stormed the Throne Room
143	She's Disqualified
146	She's Resting Now
148	So Run That You Might Obtain
150	Someone Important Has Died
152	Sorry, Ma'am, You Have the Wrong Number
156	Suddenly the Startled Couple
157	That Brother Is So Annoying
159	The Christian Gold Rush That Wasn't
162	The Closet One To Eternity Without You
164	The Heartbreak of Algebra
166	The Turning Point for Judas Iscariot

167	Then There Arose a Reasoning
169	They Won't Let Me In
172	This One Is Mine
174	Welcome o Sonic
176	Well, He Won't Be Here Tomorrow Night!
178	What's Eating You?
181	Ye Worship Ye Know Not What
183	Ye Have Not Spoken the Thing That Is Right
185	You Are Going To Get Your Purse
187	You May Have To Stay at Crete

DEDICATION

This book was written to honor the priestly prayer of Jesus recorded in John 17, which He prayed just prior to fulfilling the purpose of God in becoming the sacrificial Lamb.

In verses :8 and :20, He prayed: "For I have given them the words which thou gavest me; and they have received them..." and "Neither pray I for these alone, but for them also who shall believe on me through their word..."

In writing this book, I have given to you the words He gave to me. The stories within these pages are true. The people are real, and the events all happened. They were written, compiled, and published for your benefit. Some names have been changed.

Psalm 68:11 The Lord gave the word; great was the company of those who published it.

May God richly bless you as you walk along the pilgrim pathway.

ALL THAT GLITTERS IS NOT GOLD

It was a curious sight that caused me to wonder about its meaning. While praying one day, He opened the eyes of my heart to let me see as though I was observing from a short distance above. It was the floor of a cave illuminated by soft penetrating light from above. There were two tunnels with almost joining entrances. Neatly laid at the openings were hand tools used by miners.

I glanced to the left and noticed a small pile of "gold," and exclaimed, "Oh, that's fool's gold! I don't want that!" My attention was turned to the adjacent tunnel. That was where the true treasure was hidden, and I knew that was where I wanted to go. Although God didn't actually show who had been digging, collecting the pile of fool's gold, I concluded He was gently giving a clue that it had been me.

It has been said, "All that glitters is not gold," as a warning not to value vain pursuits. Conversely, it is also a fair warning to say, "All that is gold does not glitter." In many instances, what appears to be innocent or harmless is neither. Some things may not be attractive until their true worth is uncovered.

3rd John :9, speaks of Diotrephes "...who loveth to have the pre-eminence (Greek #5383 meaning "fond of being first, ambitious") among them." This only-mentioned-once man exhibited what has come to be known as the "Diotrephes Syndrome." Syndrome is a word meaning "a distinctive pattern of predictable behavior."

Notice that Diotrephes "loveth to have the preeminence." The word "loveth" is used here as an active present verb meaning "to thrive on." He was actively thriving on having the center stage. He had failed to receive the true meaning of the gospel. Instead, he went after "fool's gold."

Bible scholars believe the Third Epistle of John, which tells of Diotrephes, was written between A.D. 85 and A.D. 95. It is entirely possible that Diotrephes had been exposed to the teachings of Christ for some time. It appears that he didn't comprehend its true meaning.

Apostle Paul wrote to the churches in Galatia admonishing them to, "...not be desirous of vainglory." **(Galatians 5:26)** Paul also wrote to the Philippi Christians counseling them with these words, "Let nothing be done through strife or vainglory, but in lowliness of mind let each esteem others better than themselves." **(Philippians 2:3)**

When reading the carefully chosen wording the Apostle John used to describe this ambitious man, Diotrephes, we can sense his desire for control. His strategy for increasing his own status within the church was to jockey for control by slandering John. Conquering others may have been his way of hiding self-driven insecurities.

The Apostle Paul addressed a similar problem among believers at Corinth. He cautioned them in **1st Corinthians 4:6-7** with these words, "...that ye might learn in us not to think of men above that which is written, that no one of you be puffed up for one against another. For who maketh thee to differ from another?"

And, King David acknowledged, "Surely every man walketh in a vain show…" **(Psalm 39:6)**

Dear Reader, there is a secret place reserved for those who truly love God. It's a safe place. No one jockeys for position or status there. It's found at the foot of His Cross, and there is room for all. And it is there that the true gold is found.

AND, IN THE PROCESS OF TIME, IT CAME TO PASS

Five scriptures use the words, "And in the process of time it came to pass," as a bridge to cover what seems to have been a lapse of time. And, true enough, we do live our lives as a tale that is told, and our lifetimes are lived in the process of time.

The widow of Bob Sharkey was a dear friend who told of something that happened years ago when her husband attempted to do a good deed. Bob Sharkey was a retired electrician who was well known as a master craftsman in other skills, too.

A woman in Greensburg had heard of his reputation and hired him to re-paper the walls in a house she owned and planned to rent. He began the job early one morning and left in the afternoon intending to return the next morning to complete his work.

The woman came to see his workmanship. She was shocked and disappointed at what she found. The beautiful wallpaper she had chosen was riddled with wrinkles from floor to ceiling. She howled, "This is not what I wanted! This is not what I asked him to do!" And, in a fit of anger, she wrote with a bright red crayon, 'NOT ACCEPTABLE! REJECTED!" on every wall.

And, don't you know she was there waiting when Mr. Sharkey returned the next morning to finish the work he had begun. As they walked through the house together, imagine her amazement to see all the wrinkles were gone.

The paper had perfectly adhered and was all smooth and flat. Every piece had fit into place just as the master craftsman had intended, but it was all done in a process of time; a process that had to be allowed.

Mr. Sharkey recognized what had happened, and he turned to her and patiently asked, "Will you help me tear it all down, so I can begin again?"

My friend, God is just as patient with us when we don't allow the process of answered prayer. We, at times, feel tired of just working and praying. And, sometimes we don't like the temporal results.

As we are told in **Philippians 2:13**, "For it is God who <u>worketh</u> in you both to will and to do of his good pleasure." Verse 6 goes on to say, "Being confident of this very thing, that he who hath begun a good <u>work</u> in you will perform it unto the day of Christ Jesus..."

From **Ephesians 2:10**, we learn that God <u>works</u> all things after the counsel of his own will and that we are His <u>workmanship</u>. **Acts 15:18** declares, "Known unto God are all His <u>works</u> from the beginning of the world."

Be very cautious that you not limit the Holy One of Israel. He is working on your behalf, and you are always on His mind; allow Him to perfect that which concerns you, though His work is done in a "process of time."

AS SOON AS I SEE
HOW IT WILL GO WITH ME
Philippians 2:23

In approximately 60 A.D., Paul, the Apostle to the Gentiles, was in a Roman prison awaiting execution at the whim of Emperor Nero and writing to the then well-established first Christian church at Philippi.

Nero became the fifth Roman Emperor at age fifteen after his mother, Agrippina, had her husband, Claudius 1st (who was also her uncle) poisoned. Nero later murdered his mother and his second wife to please his mistress. He had an unsatisfiable and childish need for applause. He gave vocal concerts at Greek festivals and acted publicly in religious dramas, seeing himself as a religious visionary. Controlled by paranoia, he ordered a popular and successful general, Gnaeus Donitius Corbulo, to commit suicide. Nero himself would commit suicide June 9, 68 A.D. after the Roman senate declared him to be a public enemy. He had ordered Paul's execution the year prior.

QUESTION: Had the Apostle Paul been awaiting execution by the whim of Nero or martyrdom by the election of God?

When speaking to Ananias in **Acts 9:16**, the Lord said of Paul, "For I will show him how great things he must suffer for my name's sake." Some of what this writer of thirteen New Testament books was to experience in defense of the gospel are listed in **2nd Corinthians 11:24-28** and include being stoned three times, beaten with forty stripes five times, imprisoned, shipwrecked, hungry, thirsty, and cold. Yet he stated that the sufferings of this present time were not worthy to be compared with the glory that shall be revealed in us.

Do we have great faith and astonishing understanding of the things pertaining to God? We certainly have no more than the Apostle to the Gentiles, who sat in the Philippian prison and wrote, "...<u>as soon as I see how it will go with me</u>." This man of faith and power whom God had used to work miracles and who had seen people raised from the dead did not attempt to use "faith" to manipulate his circumstance. Like Paul, we will all have to wait and "see how it will go with me."

It is believed that 2nd Peter was written six years after Paul's martyrdom. His epistles were recognized even then as having scriptural authority. Peter wrote of Paul's epistles and said:

2nd Peter 3:16 ...which they that are unlearned and unstable wrest, <u>as they do also the other scriptures</u>...

Waiting before the Lord is a privilege. Why not enjoy your time of waiting as He demonstrates His faithfulness? After all, most of our lifetimes are spent waiting before Him.

BE CAREFUL WHICH RUTS YOU CHOOSE

Many years ago, a sign which read, "Be careful which ruts you choose. You are going to be in them for the next 2,000 miles," was posted over the entrance to the Oregon Trail at Independence, Missouri.

This famous 2,000 mile trail winds through the six states of Missouri, Kansas, Nebraska, Wyoming, Idaho, and Oregon. Explorers began blazing its paths as early as 1742 followed by the famous Lewis and Clark expedition of 1804.

The journey generally took four to six months to complete and was fraught with many hardships resulting from poor equipment, attacks by Native Americans, and illness. Many emigrant pilgrims died on their journey as cholera ravaged the caravans. Treasured items could be seen jettisoned (tossed aside) to lighten heavy loads. Just as the ship's tackling had to be tossed overboard on the ship carrying the prisoner Paul to Rome. **(Acts 28:19)**

In some places, ruts were carved wagon wheel deep by the caravans. They are left as a silent reminder of the hardships experienced by the pilgrims. Once a path was chosen, it was almost impossible to change to another.

This can also be true regarding the paths we choose in our lifetimes. **Proverbs 2:13** warns of those, "who leave the paths of uprightness to walk in the ways of darkness." **Proverbs 3:6** states, "In all your ways acknowledge him, and he will direct your paths." Verse :17 of the same chapter speaks of wisdom and understanding saying,

"Her ways are ways of pleasantness, and all her paths are peace."

We learn from modern day shepherds that sheep, <u>when left to themselves</u>, continue to trod the same paths over and over. These paths can become shoulder deep ruts filled with rainwater and mud. What misery the sheep are in when their wool becomes clogged with mud and debris. They become helpless victims of the paths they have chosen. My friend, follow the Good Shepherd, and He will lead you in paths of righteousness for His name's sake. **(Psalm 23:3)**

Jeremiah 6:16 admonishes us to, "… ask for the old paths, where is a good way, and walk therein, and ye shall find rest for your souls."

Throughout your lifetime, be careful and prayerful concerning which paths you choose. After all, you may be in them for a long time.

BE IT UNTO ME ACCORDING TO THY WORD

The first two chapters of the Gospel of Luke are two of the most beautiful and revealing chapters in the entire Bible. Notice the response of the young virgin Mary as she surrenders to the startling news of Gabriel informing her that she would become the Messiah's mother. Mary's response recorded in Luke 1:38 revealed her heart. She said, "Behold, the handmaiden of the Lord; be it unto me according to thy word."

Consider also the words of her cousin Elizabeth, in verse :45, as she said, "And blessed is she that believed; for there shall be a performance of those things which were told her of the Lord."

Job 23:10, 13, 14 record the words of Job as he said, "But he knoweth the way that I take, when he hath tried (tested) me, I shall come forth as gold. But he is of one mind, and he performeth the thing that is appointed for me; and many such things are with him."

Mary, Elizabeth, and Job could not have dreamed of the things that He had appointed (purposed) for their lives. But they loved Him enough to yield and to allow Him to perform His great and eternal purposes.

He offers you the privilege of doing the same today and every day. He will move you toward your appointed destiny as you daily yield to Him.

Isaiah 55:8-9 For my thoughts are not your thoughts, neither are your ways my ways, saith the Lord. For as the heavens are higher than the earth, so are my ways higher than your ways, and my thoughts than your thoughts.

Jeremiah 29:11 For I know the thoughts I think toward you, saith the Lord, thoughts of peace, and not of evil, to give you an expected end.

How many times have you come to the conclusion of something and thought, "This is sure not what I expected." In the end, all that will really matter is that He <u>performed</u> His <u>purpose</u> and that things turned out as He desired.

BE NOT AS THE OSTRICH

Job 39:14-17 tells of the ostrich "which leaveth her eggs in the earth, and warmeth them in dust, and forgetteth that the foot may crush them, or that the wild beast may break them. She is hardened against her young ones, as though they were not hers; her labor is in vain without fear, <u>because</u> God hath deprived her of wisdom, neither hath He imparted understanding."

Why would such a frivolous scripture be included in the Holy Word of God? Notice that two Creator-omitted essential ingredients cause the ostrich's tragic actions. God had deprived her of wisdom and understanding. Herein lies the problem for the ostrich and for mankind, as well. Surely, you will read in tomorrow's newspaper the tragic actions of those who lack wisdom and understanding.

Let's ponder a scripture found in **Psalm 119:73**:
Thy hands have made me and fashioned me; give me understanding, that I may learn thy commandments.

The first eight words form a complete sentence whose truth is easily agreed upon. Just knowing that His hands have made and fashioned us is satisfying. Oh, but wait, the psalmist then asked for something he lacked. "Give me understanding, that I may learn thy commandments," is a plea from the heart of someone who recognized he is lacking something essential; something that his Creator purposefully omitted.

This obviously puts man in the dilemma of wanting to obey God's commandments but of lacking the wisdom and understanding to do so.

And notice how the heart of the Apostle Paul exploded in wonderment as he exclaimed in **Romans 11:33**, "Oh, the depth of the riches both of the wisdom and knowledge of God! How unsearchable are his judgments, and his ways are past finding out!

What a relief to follow the direction given to believers and recorded in **James 1:5** which states, "If any of you lack wisdom, let him ask of God, who giveth to all men liberally, and upbraideth not, and it shall be given him."

All the wisdom and understanding needed by man is given in abundance to those who ask it of Him. Here's another truth to bring comfort to your soul. Our adversary, the devil, who is also a created being, is totally void of the wisdom and understanding of God.

1st Corinthians 2:8 speaks of the hidden wisdom of God and says, "Which none of the princes of this world (age) knew; for had they known it, they would not have crucified the Lord of glory."

If the devil had had access to the hidden wisdom of God, he never would have crucified the Lord of glory. Further good news is that saints walking in the wisdom and understanding of God can never be out-witted by the devil working through others who aren't.

BECOMING A RHODES SCHOLAR

A Rhodes scholarship is an international post-graduate award for study at the University of Oxford in Oxford, England. It is the world's oldest and most prestigious international scholarship having begun in 1904.

In 1946, former U.S. President Jimmy Carter, as a scholarship applicant, completed a series of interviews. One such interview was scheduled with a university professor. Arriving on time for the interview, he knocked on the professor's office door and heard a gruff voice growl, "Come in." As he entered, the professor did not rise to greet him, but instead remained seated at his desk with his back toward him.

The professor may have been "educated beyond his intelligence," as some would say. Or maybe he was impressed with his perception of his importance. Whatever the cause, he remained in this detached position throughout the lopsided interview. By the time the interview neared completion, the then-twenty-two year old Jimmy Carter's confidence had been shredded.

Referring to his undergraduate studies, the professor questioned, "Did you do your best?" It was a sobering inquiry to which he could only answer, "No, sir, I didn't." The professor's only remaining query was, "Why not?" The then-young Jimmy Carter paused before stating his self-incriminating reason, "I was distracted."

The interview concluded with the professor remaining blasé and the applicant feeling dejected. He was not to win the scholarship he had desired.

God spoke through the prophet Jeremiah to pronounce judgment upon His people for their choice of forsaking Him after He had offered mercy.

Jeremiah 18:17 I will scatter them as with an east wind before the enemy; <u>I will show them the back, and not the face</u>, in the day of their calamity.

What a dreadful, despairing condition to be in. And to think it was all their choosing. Earlier in verse :12, after being urged by God to "... return, now, everyone from his evil way, and make your ways and your doings good," they sealed their fate by declaring, "There is no hope, but we will every one do the imagination of his evil heart."

The Apostle Paul wrote to the believers in Thessalonica stressing the seriousness of serving God in sincerity. The beginning words of **1st Thessalonians 2:4** provide food for thought, "But as we were <u>allowed</u> of God to be put in trust with the gospel ..." This only-used-once Bible word "<u>allowed</u>" (Greek #1381) means "to be approved." What a thought and what a responsibility! The only question is, what will we do with that trust we have been <u>allowed</u> to have? Will we <u>allow</u> distractions to disqualify us from obtaining God's acceptance?

The words of Jesus recorded in **Luke 21:34-36** offer a stern warning that our hearts not be "overcharged with surfeiting." Surfeiting is another used-only-once Bible word, and it means (Greek #2897) "headaches caused by excess." We certainly do live in a day when hearts are being overcharged with surfeiting. Many hearts become "overcharged" by <u>surf</u>ing the world-wide-web and leaving little room for thoughts of God.

The entire text reads as follows:
Luke 21:34-36 And take heed to yourselves, lest at any time your hearts be overcharged with surfeiting, and drunkenness, and cares of this life, and so that day come upon you unawares. For like a snare shall it come on all them that dwell on the face of the earth. Watch, ye, therefore, and pray always, that ye may be accounted worthy to escape all these things that shall come to pass, and to stand before the Son of man.

In today's world, we are plagued by distractions caused by constant media bombardment. We must guard our heart and home at all times against ungodly intrusions. As our society drifted from God, it became an activity-centered culture preoccupied with sinful pleasures rather than His Holy presence.

Chances are you are not focused on becoming a Rhodes Scholar. I hope you are focused on being a sincere Christian who guards against distractions. Yes, that task is a battle. But, it's a battle worth fighting and winning, when you consider the enormous eternal consequences.

BETWEEN THE PROMISE AND THE FULFILLMENT

Between the promise of God and the fulfillment is a space of time called misery. The duration of your season of misery depends, in part, by your willingness to learn the ways of God and to glorify Him through it all. Many necessary attributes are acquired during this crucial segment of your journey.

M Mary experienced many miseries between the time Gabriel spoke awesome promises to her and the resurrection of Jesus.
I Isaiah wept in misery years before his martyrdom over the sins of the Lord's chosen people.
S Sarah walked the painful path of unbelief until God performed His word to her.
E Ezekiel endured hardship and misery as he spoke God's word to a sin-laden backslidden people.
R Rebekah traveled the lonely road of bareness as she waited for God to fulfill her desire.
Y You, too, may experience prolonged times physical and spiritual fatigue as you struggle to hold onto what God has promised.

2nd Samuel 22:31 states plainly, "As for God, his way is perfect; the word of the Lord is tried (tested); he is a shield to all them that trust in him."

Psalm 12:6 divulges this truth, "The words of the Lord are pure words, like silver tried (tested) in a furnace of earth, purified seven times."

Hearing Him speak directly to you causes you to embark on a walk of faith. Your belief in those words will be tested many times. Hopefully, you will say with confidence, like **Job (23:10)**, "But he knoweth the way that I take; when he hath tested me, I shall come forth as gold."

Hebrews 10:38 teaches us, "Now the just shall live by faith; but if any man draw back, my soul shall have no pleasure in him."

As you journey through your time of misery, you may be encouraged to know you are not alone in your season of waiting on the fulfillment.

These words are written in the hope of inspiring you to continue your walk of faith knowing full well that the eternal rewards will be well worth it.

BIRD, YOUR DAYS ARE NUMBERED!

It would be wonderful if every neighborhood had a man like the one known as "Dear Herman," whose actual name was Herman Dier. In our part of the world, this family name is sometimes pronounced as "Di-er" and at other times as "Dear." As this man became dear to me, I began to simply call him "Dear Herman."

Herman and I met September 2, 1990, the day I first saw the arboretum-like property adjacent to his on Cassle Road. We met at his driveway at the end of the seldom-traveled dirt/gravel road when he inquired if there was anything I needed. I told him that I was looking for land to build a house. To my relief, he didn't seem to mind the thought of having a neighbor invade his solitude.

We found a realtor's "For Sale" sign fallen and mostly covered with weeds. Arrangements were made through the realtor who represented the landowner in another state, and I purchased the wooded 2.3 acres. After the house plans were drawn, it was time to begin building. Only how could that be accomplished when I knew I lacked the ability to build a house, and much less to do so while working fulltime? I couldn't see that happening. At least I knew enough to know I didn't know what I was doing and that I needed a lot of help.

Three times I thought I had located a man who could serve as an overseer for the project. But none of my plans worked. There was no one to help. I well remember lying on my bed at night looking up in the darkness with a heavier-than-lead fear knot sitting in my chest. I prayed,

"Lord, come and let us reason together. You created me; therefore You know that I cannot do this, right? Therefore, You will not require it of me, right?" (Wrong!)

He remained silent as I drifted off into a troubled sleep awakening the next morning with the ever-present fear knot. Yes, I know that the Bible tells us sixty-two times to "fear not." However, for me, building a house was like entering an unknown zone while toting this "fear knot."

The day carpenters were scheduled to begin the framework, I wondered if they were on the job. I called Dear Herman from work and asked if he would mind looking over to see if there were any carpenters on the property.

He excitedly spoke, "My carpenters were here, but now my carpenters are gone. I don't know where my carpenters are." At that moment the fear knot left my heart. Dear Herman had stepped up to the plate and assumed the position of overseer. And what an outstanding overseer he was!

Among the many things he did to assist the building was to take down his fence so multitudes of workers could access my wooded property through his. He stayed on the job day and night six days a week overseeing everything. God amazed me as I saw Him use this wonderful man to meet my need.

Dear Herman was known not to tolerate anything that didn't operate like it was supposed to. Whatever item didn't work and couldn't be repaired was discarded. Once a decision was made, he never looked back.

He bought a parrot at a garage sale and placed it in its cage on his screened back porch. Oh, how he enjoyed that talkative bird! He even taught him to say, "Herman," which he called out constantly. One Saturday as I was working outside, I bent over to disconnect a water hose. I heard that bird calling, "Herbert! Herbert! Herbert!"
By this time, I had gotten to know Dear Herman fairly well. I spoke out loud, "Bird, your days are numbered."

The following week I mentioned to Dear Herman that I hadn't heard his parrot in a few days. "Aw, that bird! He couldn't even remember my name, so I got rid of him," was his reply. This good-as-gold neighbor wouldn't put up with a bird that he had purchased, fed, housed, and protected but that didn't remember his name.

These words of lamentation spoken by God, our Father, were written in:
Isaiah 1:2-3 Hear, O heavens, and give ear O earth; for the Lord hath spoken: I have nourished and brought up children, and they have rebelled against me. The ox knoweth his owner, and the ass, his master's crib, but Israel doth not know, my people doth not consider.

He again revealed His disappointment and heartache in **Jeremiah 2:32** by lamenting, "Yet my people have forgotten me days without number."

The following is a portion of a prayer of Moses recorded in Psalm Ninety, the only psalm ascribed to him. After he expressed how futile the sum of our lives can be, he added, "So teach us to number our days, that we may apply our hearts unto wisdom."

If you are reading these words, then you are alive and have God-given opportunity to remember Him and to apply your heart unto His wisdom.

Just as Dear Herman's parrot soon became history, so will we.

James 4:14 Whereas ye know not what shall be on the morrow. For what is your life? It is even a vapor that appears for a little time and then vanished away.

BRIAN HAD BEEN JERKED, POPPED, AND SLAPPED

Brian Collier had been jerked, popped, and slapped by the best of the best ministers and yet no remedy was found for his chronic debilitating back pain. For five l-o-n-g years, his name had been on the prayer list of a number of churches and ministries and yet no relief was obtained. Neither had any medical exam revealed the cause. It would be an understatement to say that his perplexing predicament vexed his soul.

Following Brian's ministering in a Sunday morning church service where others were healed of physical ailments, the entire congregation witnessed him hobbling off the podium platform and everyone wondered at the pitiful sight.

However, the straw that broke the camel's back (also known as "the last straw") was placed on Brian during lunch with the church's pastor that day. As Brian grimaced in pain, the pastor leaned across the table and crossed the boundaries of friendship by launching a gossip-driven probe as he inquired, "Brian, you know we have been friends for a long time. Why don't you just tell me what the besetting sin is?" This pastor's intrusive question may not have been asked out of concern as much as it was to obtain fresh fodder to fuel a judgmental spirit. Brian's momentary knee-jerk reaction was stymied by the disheartening realization that his long-time pastor friend wasn't his long-time pastor friend. He later stated that this pastor would never know just how close he came to receiving a knuckle-sandwich along with his lunch.

Weeks after Brian's luncheon inquisition, he began being bothered by a lump on the back of his neck that had been there for quite some time. He made a doctor's appointment for a routine exam. His physician wasn't overly concerned but did order a biopsy.

Brian reported to the clinic where the biopsy was to be performed and was met by a physician and his assistant. He was then made comfortable in a treatment room where an anesthetic was administered.

Brian remained in a semi-conscience fog while the physician made a small incision to provide an inside view of the lump. "Oooo, that's ugly," commented the assistant, while the physician concluded, "We'd better not touch it." Then they woke him up to tell him what he had just heard. ☺

An appointment was made with a specialist who successfully removed what turned out to be a benign growth. And, to Brian's utter amazement and relief, the lump's removal also removed the unexplained pain.

Just as Job remained faithful to God while suffering unexplained devastating pain and losses; Brian had remained steadfast in the Lord. And as scripture states, (Job 1:22,) "In all this Job sinned not, nor charged God foolishly." Brian had remained faithful to God throughout his trial-without-answers, too.

What about the pastor with the whetted accusation-appetite? **Matthew 7:1-2** records the words of Jesus warning, "Judge not, that ye be not judged. For with what judgment ye judge, ye shall be judged …"

And **Romans 8:33** clearly states, "Who shall lay anything to the charge of God's elect. It is God that justifieth."

BUT I DIDN'T BRING ANYBODY WITH ME!

Dwight L. Moody was preaching a revival meeting in Chicago the night of the infamous "Chicago Fire" October 8, 1871. The fire left 90,000 people homeless and 250 dead as it destroyed a four square mile area.

As the fire spread, those who could ran to the river where Brother Moody had joined with others who were relaying them across to safety. Those who were fearful had to be thrown in had in to escape death. Brother Moody reached out and grabbed a young frightened girl whom he could not console. He tried to reassure her by telling her that she was safe, that she would make it to the other side, and that the smoke and flames could not come to where she was going. Between heart wrenching sobs, she stammered, "I know I'm safe, but I didn't bring anybody with me!"

True believers know that they are safe, that they have been rescued, that the smoke and flames won't come to where they are going. But knowing this is not enough. We don't want to leave this life knowing that we have not brought anyone with us. Scripture tells us, "A true witness delivereth souls ..." **(Proverbs 14:25)**

Remember **2nd Corinthians 5:18** tells us, "And all things are of God, who hath reconciled us to Himself by Jesus Christ, and hath given us the ministry of reconciliation."

He will enable you to "bring someone with you" as you continue in faithfulness to Him.

BY LITTLE AND LITTLE

The Bible speaks of "the hidden wisdom of God" **(1st Corinthians 2:7)** and tells us plainly in **Proverbs 25:2**, "It is the glory of God to conceal a thing, but the honor of kings is to search out a matter."

Let's search out the hidden wisdom of God and determine why He may withhold a "good thing" even though His word promises, "No good thing will I withhold from them who walketh uprightly." **(Psalm 84:11)**

And, as Gideon, you may ask during your earthly sojourning, "... if the Lord be with us, why then is all this befallen us? And where are all the miracles which our fathers told us of ..." **(Judges 6:13)**

Exodus 23 tells of the wisdom of God in sending an angel to bring His people into the land of the Amorites, the Hittites, the Perizzites, the Canaanites, the Hivites, and the Jebusites.

Wow! He knowingly sent them into the lands of six enemies as part of His curriculum designed for their perfection. They were to learn not to compromise with heathen people and to become strong enough to possess the land for His glory.

Notice in verse: 26, God, when referring to the territory to be conquered said, "thy land," as though it was already in their possession.

Verses :28-30 reveal His hidden wisdom, "And I will send hornets (large, savage species of wasp) before thee, which shall drive out the Hivite, the Canaanite, and the Hittite from before thee. I will not drive them out from before thee in one year; lest the land become desolate and the beasts of the field multiply against thee. By little and little I will drive them out from before thee, until thou be increased, and inherit the land."

Symbolically, the phrase "the beast(s) of the field," which the Bible mentions forty times, can mean the pride, arrogance, or haughtiness that plaques fallen man. We need to guard constantly against these attitudes of the heart.

The Gospel of Mark lists thirteen things that come from the heart of man that cause defilement:
Mark 7:21-22 For from within, out of the heart of men, proceed evil thoughts, adulteries, fornications, murders, thefts, covetousness, wickedness, deceit, lasciviousness, an evil eye, blasphemy, pride, foolishness. All these evil things come from within, and defile the man.

Knowing the dangers, God wants us to learn to walk circumspectly and to increase "by little and little." He knows how quickly the "beasts of the field" can multiply and conquer His people.

The first mention of this term, "beast of the field," is found in Genesis.

Genesis 3:1 Now the serpent was more subtle (Hebrew #6175 meaning, "cunning") than any beast of the field ...

The serpent then proceeded to seduce Eve by enticing her through pride; one of the thirteen things Mark lists as causing defilement.

Now that we have gained insight into the language of God, the hidden wisdom of God is not-so-hidden. We can clearly understand and appreciate His wisdom stated in:

Deuteronomy 7:22 And the Lord thy God will put out these nations before thee <u>by little and little</u>; thou mayest not consume them at once, lest <u>the beasts of the field</u> increase upon thee.

My friend be content in your walk with the Lord knowing that He will give you the increase but it may be little by little as a way of protecting you.

COURTHOUSE EXPERIENCES

As a sure way of insuring a rewarding day, I prayed that God would use me to be the answer to someone's prayer.

It was just about dark-thirty when I reached the foot of the courthouse steps on my way to conduct an evening tour of the Clerk of Court's office for a group of law students. From the bottom step upward, I stepped in sort of a crisscross manner slicing across the stack of wide steps.

I glanced toward the main doors as a large group of people began to spill out. I had seen this happen before and concluded that a trial had ended and that these folks were glad to be tumbling out of there.

Before I could step aside, I collided with a woman. Our bodies abruptly bumped together. Then, before I could mutter an apology, she collapsed sobbing into my arms. She was a slender well-dressed black woman. I held her close to me as she told of just leaving court after seeing her son convicted of robbery. She was too distraught to even hold her head up. Her grief and torment were too much for her to bear. God had put us on a collision course and provided an opportunity for me to be the answer to her prayer for compassion and strength. I held her body up while we prayed on the courthouse steps. I felt the strength of the Lord flow through me as it infused her.

A moment later, she was one her way, and I was on mine. God had answered both our prayers in a way that only He could.

On another occasion and near dark-thirty again, I was galloping to the courthouse on the sidewalk nearby. I looked up just in time to see four worn-to–a-frazzle attorneys marching in unison side by side shoulder-to-shoulder wearing business suits covered by overcoats.
The three men and one woman brigade all stared down at the sidewalk as they tromped. The atmosphere surrounding them was heavy. A short distance away, I could feel their weary exhaustion.

Just prior to our passing one another, I spoke up and interjected, "I am sorry you lost." Without missing a step in their fatigued march, they turned to me with expressionless drained faces and chimed, "WE WON!"

I have thought about this brief encounter many times because it reminds me of weary Christian soldiers. Even though we win the battle, it doesn't mean that we won't be frazzled and exhausted when the day is done.

Isaiah 9:5 For every battle of the warrior is with confused noise, and garments rolled in blood.

This scripture gives fair warning to those entering the arena of Christendom. Before entering the battle, determine within your heart to be the warrior God needs you to be.

Then came a day when I had gotten to work before realizing I had forgotten to eat breakfast. Suddenly I felt that I needed to eat something right away. I glanced at the wall clock and could hardly believe that it was only ten after eleven. I knew it wouldn't matter when I took my lunch break, so I headed on down to the employee break room.

Two Christian women were there when I entered. One was very downcast and was saying how she didn't know how she was going to make it. They didn't mind me hearing their conversation, so I listened.

The troubled woman was saying how her brother-in-law had lost his job in Detroit and that he, his wife, and their children had moved in with her, her husband, and children. She knew these relatives were in a hard place, and she wanted to be of help. However, her wagon was already loaded with working fulltime, caring for her husband, children, and needs of her household.

Neither had asked for my advice, but I spoke quoting a scripture familiar to them. I said, "Oh, only a vessel of honor is fit for the Master's use. You are a chosen vessel unto Him, and He is using you to bless this family in need." Hearing this truth exclaimed did not seem to have an effect on her despair at that moment. However, the next time I saw this lovely Christian woman, she was beaming as she told me that every day, when she got home from work, her sister-in-law had the house clean, laundry done, and a tasty supper on the stove.

My friend, when God uses us to bless others, we cannot help but be blessed in return.

DADDY, YOU'LL NEVER BE ASHAMED OF ME AGAIN

It was almost midnight when we left the house and headed to the hospital to be by the pastor's side. Brother Don's wife had called saying they had received the phone call every parent dreads. Their oldest son had been in a horrible accident caused by a drunk driver.

Brother Don had left for the hospital while his wife stayed home with younger sleeping children. I called church members who rushed to their home.

The hospital physician waited until we arrived to tell the father that his son had died. My husband then entered the examining room with Brother Don to view his son's lifeless body. Stunning shockwaves swept over his body, soul, and spirit as he tried to comprehend that his oldest son was gone. He collapsed into my husband's arms.

There's nothing as final as death and nothing more horrific than losing a child that you had a tumultuous relationship with. Don, Jr., whom everyone called Donnie, was gone. His father would never hear his voice again, or so he thought.

My husband drove Brother Don in his truck while I followed in our van to his house which was now filled with dazed relatives and friends. Sadness had draped their home like a tarp.

In the days that followed, it was learned that the uninjured driver of the other vehicle had been charged with DWI, Vehicle Homicide, Speeding, and Failure to

Stop at an Intersection. It was also learned that this same driver had caused the death of his own brother two years prior while driving intoxicated. What a tragedy that he was still drinking and still driving.

Donnie's death happened on the same road as the location of his father's church. In fact, as men were standing outside the church talking after that Sunday evening's service, two racing trucks flew by. One of the church members pointed to the lead truck and said, "That guy is going to kill someone!" Sure enough, about seven miles up the highway, the lead truck collided with the truck driven by Donnie, killing him upon impact.

As my mind pieced together recent memories of Donnie, I was encouraged remembering that he had once more made a firm commitment to live for God. I had seen him kneeling at the church altar and praying in deep contrition at the close of a Sunday evening service. I interceded for him while kneeling on the opposite side of the altar but without touching him. He was emptying his heart before God, and I wanted to be careful not to intrude. I knew what a struggle he had had with booze and illicit drugs. He had even been in prison for a few years as a result of following in the same youthful missteps his father had taken. I waited until his burden began to ease. I knew he would know my voice without seeing my face, so I put my arms gently around him and spoke softly into his ear. As he listened, the liberating words from God's heart provided the needed anchor of assurance. You know, sometimes God will "read your mail" through someone else, and you know that it is God speaking.

I remember telling him that even though he had a "Jr." after his name that he wasn't a ditto or a clone and that God loved him as an individual. I told him that God was proud of him and knew that he had allowed Him to bring him a long, long way. I told him that God was not disappointed in him or ashamed of him. Donnie believed these words. He left the altar a new man. There was a visible change in his countenance. This brief exchange was a golden moment in his life.

Donnie was to meet his Maker a few weeks later while still enjoying the release from guilt, defeat, and shame. It was as though God had determined to rescue him at his strongest point before he might possibly be overwhelmed again by the snares of this life.

His mother later confided something to me. Her heart was heavy with the memories of unresolved conflict between her husband and his son. She had witnessed the tirade of harmful insults that her husband had spewed upon him. She said he had told him that he was a failure, that he was disappointed in him, and that he was ashamed of him. Perhaps the father's intense emotion was caused by him being afraid of his son continuing to make the same mistakes he had made earlier in his own life.

I sighed deeply as she shared the depth of their family's dysfunction. I mused in my mind wondering if I would have allowed God to use me at the altar encouraging Donnie had I known what his mother was now revealing.

Several books have been written entitled, "Famous Last Words," containing the last words of dying clergymen, movie stars, presidents, military commanders, and ordinary people. I've read one of these books and found the sentiments of dying people to be as varied as the people themselves.

Some died praising God while others died cursing Him. Some died mocking the "afterlife" as though it was a fantasy, while still others expressed delight to be entering eternity trusting in the Lord.

God made sure that Donnie would leave his own "Famous Last Words." His father, days after his funeral, heard a message from him that he had left on his phone recorder the day before his death. With a made up mind and a determined heart, Donnie had spoken these words, "Daddy, you'll never be ashamed of me again. I'm a new man, and I'm living for God. I love you, Daddy.

DEAR ABBY, I AM A CHRISTIAN

These words caught my eye while reading the newspaper, "Dear Abby, I am a Christian." I blinked and wondered why anyone identifying himself as a Christian would be seeking counsel from a newspaper advice columnist and especially one known for ungodly counsel. It's sad to say that this person had not experienced Jesus in ways He intended.

Let's leave that sad thought for a moment and look at some familiar nouns that end with the letter "r." Nouns ending in "r" identify exactly who or what a person is. Words like:

doctor	lawyer	murderer
teacher	painter	preacher
banker	janitor	realtor
soldier	roofer	liar

Remember that nouns ending with the letter "r" are exact. A person may tell a lie but that doesn't make him a "liar." A liar is someone who constantly and habitually lies.

Now, let's look at some nouns ending in "r" the Bible uses to tell us exactly who Jesus is and who He wants to be in our lives. Words like:

Creator	Deliverer	Author
Finisher	Redeemer	Savior
Governor	Intercessor	Master
Mediator	Healer	Counselor

What do you need Jesus to be in your life today at this very moment? Choose from one of the twelve nouns listed above or add some of your own. The point is that we don't need counsel from a newspaper advice columnist when His name is Counselor. Learn who He is as you are learning who you are in Him.

Sometimes when I awake in the morning and even before getting out of bed, I greet Him by saying, "Good morning, Governor," as a way of acknowledging that He is Zion's righteous Governor, as well as the Governor of my life.

Doing this marks the beginning of a beautiful day with my Savior who is my Creator, Deliverer, Mediator, Master, Healer, Redeemer, Intercessor, Counselor, Author, and Finisher.

So, pour out your heart to Him who is all things and who wants to become all things to you. You might save the time of writing a letter as well as the cost of a postage stamp.

DON'T BECOME AN OXYMORON

We use expressions without considering that they may be contradictory. Modern day language can be spotted with an unnoticed oxymoron like:

exact estimate

freezer burn

clearly confused

unbiased opinion

open secret

"Oxymoron" comes from two Greek words; "oxys" meaning sharp or keen and "moros" which means foolish. An oxymoron can be sharp and keen, but at the same time foolish.

Psalm 115:17 The dead praise not the Lord, neither any that go down into silence.

Certainly, no one wants to "go down into silence," and especially since there is a deafening silence in the realm of the dead.

Deciding to accept the Blood sacrifice of Jesus as your propitiation, may be the only choice you'll never regret making. That thought may be old news, but it's still the Good News (gospel) from God to man.

Live your life not as an oxymoron but as a reflection of Christ abiding in you. Don't let the tale of your life be a genuine imitation.

After all, those who miss the purpose of God in creating them, may be found missing when the Lamb opens the Book of Life. **(Revelation 3:5)**

FATHER, I NEED TO TELL YOU SOMETHING

"Father, I need to tell you something that You already know," were the words that began my prayer. I was sitting in my car after the Sunday morning church service and feeling like the poster-child of church-hoppers. I continued, "You know that I didn't receive a thing in the morning service. There's nothing for me here from You."

I hung my head as I continued speaking in textbook reality, "I don't remember what the sermon was about. I can't recall one scripture the pastor used." It was an alarming realization followed by, "Lord, I gotta get out of here."

Later, the scripture came to mind, "... when they were come from Bethany, he (Jesus) was hungry." **(Mark 11:12)** I knew I was hungry. If being hungry for more of God meant finding another church, then so be it. I guess it was coincidental that the church I was leaving was named "Bethany." ☺

Church experience can be more of an arena than a utopian grazing ground. I was to learn that a woman alone could be high on the food chain of men seeking ego-driven dominion fueled by predator instincts. Nevertheless, following God's curriculum for me, I was also to learn that He would fight my battles.

My Father had ordained that I travel the scenic route on my journey to the glory world. And what a journey it has been! Nevertheless, like the song written by The Goodmans, "I Wouldn't Take Nothing For My Journey

Now." He caused me to grow at an exponential rate, which has seemed like a snail's pace at times to me.

Believers who launch out on a walk of faith will suffer from the loss of innocence that comes with it. It is like seeing the unvarnished version of "romance verse reality." Yes, at my Father's direction, I have changed churches. However, I have never once backed-up or changed Gods.

Lambs are infamous for eating the roots of vegetation leaving no chance for new growth of future food. The all-knowing Good Shepherd must rotate their grazing in order to insure their future health and well-being.

I have learned to trust His decisions on where I am to graze in His field. These words are written to encourage you to do the same.

FRANK AND DORIS COMMAND MONEY

There it was printed plainly on their personal check, "Frank and Doris command money to come to them, in Jesus' name." I read the eye-popping phrase that seemed to jump off their five dollar offering check while preparing the church bank deposit. It would have been amusing had it not been so sad. It was sad for Frank and Doris who, though called by His name, clearly did not know Him the way He wants to be known.

It was also sad for God who has since creation continually spoken His desire to be intimately known by man. However, since creation, man has had the prevalent propensity to "shape God in his own image."

Frank and Doris would have been hard-pressed to find a scriptural basis for commanding money, much less to do so "in Jesus' name." However, the Bible is replete with scriptures assuring believers that God will supply their every need.

This couple had been ensnared by a tactic of Satan without even knowing they had become prisoners of war. Their focus had been diverted from living a holy life separate unto God to serving the "little g" God of this world. This "little g" God is filthy. "Filthy lucre" is mentioned five times in the New Testament. And, if it was filthy then, think of what is today. According to a news report, a survey conducted in 2009 found 90 percent of U.S. currency was laced with cocaine. Now that's filthy!

The young Timothy was warned by the Apostle Paul in **1st Timothy 6:9**, "But they that will (desire) to be rich fall into temptation and a snare, and into many foolish and hurtful lusts, which drown men in destruction and perdition."

Remember, too, that in the Parable of the Sower, Jesus warned, "...the deceitfulness of riches, choke the word, and he (the hearer) becometh unfruitful." **Luke 8:5-18**
The sixth chapter of Matthew is peppered with words such as: "Ye cannot serve God and mammon." In the book of Acts, the apostles used the phrase, "in the name of Jesus" five times but never once was it used to "command money." On one occasion the Apostle Paul, being grieved, turned to a woman who had followed him speaking religious jargon, and he spoke to the spirit controlling her, "I command thee, <u>in the name of Jesus</u> Christ, to come out of her." **(Acts 16:18)**

A "Christian" who is motivated by greed and who gives in order to receive is one who does not understand the God they say they are serving. And delving into realms not provided for at Calvary is to teeter on the tightrope of presumption.

Gauging from the proclamation Frank and Doris chose to have printed on their five dollar offering check, it is obvious that they had not read or understood many New Testament scriptures.

Here's one found in **2nd Corinthians 9:6** that they evidently overlooked, "He who soweth sparingly shall also reap sparingly; and he who soweth bountifully shall reap also bountifully.

GARMENTS ROLLED IN BLOOD

Isaiah 9:5 is not an ideal scripture to use when encouraging someone to serve the Lord; because it says, "For every battle of the warrior is with confused noise, and garments rolled in blood ..."

Battlefields are full of bloody bodies. Many of those are killed by what is known as "friendly-fire," meaning their own comrades mistakenly killed them. It is estimated that forty percent of our casualties in the Vietnam War were a result of "friendly fire." The "friendly fire" casualties in God's army are also extremely high.

1st Corinthians 14:33 For God is not the author of confusion, but of peace ...

James 3:16 For where envying and strife are, there is confusion and every evil work.

When you sense confusion, step aside and ask God to remove it or remove you. By being aware of your surroundings, you'll avoid many hurtful snares.

Gideon's unarmed army of men was reduced by 22,000 who were disqualified by being fearful; another 10,000 were then eliminated for the same reason; leaving a mere 300 to defeat the enemies of God. **(Judges 7:2-7)**

If you were to ask any of the remaining three hundred, "Well, how did you do on your test today?" Certainly all would say, "What test? I don't know anything about a test. I was just doing the best I could." Isn't that what we are all expected to do? Just go on with the help of God, and do the best you can.

Gideon's unarmed army was chosen based on their individual reaction to adversity. These courageous men were unaccustomed to battle. Armed only with lanterns and trumpets, Gideon instructed his army to "Look on me and do likewise." **(Judges 7:17)**

Gideon's counsel to, "Look on me and do likewise" is still valid today for those who are walking with Jesus. And yes, there was confused noise and garments rolled in blood because "the Lord had set every man's sword against his fellow." All of this was accomplished according to the promise God had spoken earlier to Gideon. **(Judges 6:14)**

   Judges 7:9 Arise, get thee down unto the host; for I have delivered (past tense) it into thy hand.

Be courageous in your life's battles knowing that the God who never fails is with you. Always choose God's path, plan, and purpose. You won't be disappointed, and you won't be ashamed on Judgment Day. Keep in mind that heaven is your destination and to be like Jesus is your goal. We must never lose sight of His great eternal rewards. Regardless of the personal cost, the rewards will be worth it.

GASSED TOMATOES AREN'T THAT TASTY

Have you ever wondered why the ripe-looking grocery store tomatoes are virtually tasteless? While their reddish color indicates ripeness, the proof is in the pudding, so to speak. One disappointing bite lets the eater know the Creator-ordained maturing process has been circumvented by the modern technology of "gassing." A sensory plummet and perhaps a groan or two follows the first bite. The diner may be correctly thinking, "They just don't make tomatoes like they used to."

Nowadays, picked-green tomatoes are stacked on pallets in large ripening rooms to "color up" their outward appearance. They are gassed for three days with ethylene, which triggers the production of enzymes that produce the artificial red color causing the ripened appearance.

All plants need nitrogen enriched soil in which to grow. Whereas air is 78 percent nitrogen, it is not in a form usable by plants. God sees to it that lightning five times hotter than the sun's surface strikes the earth 8,640,000 times a day, and changes the nitrogen in air into a form plants can use.

The Creator-ordained ripening process requires the tomato to remain attached to the vine, which is drawing God-supplied nitrogen from the soil. Ripening by the sun gives them a higher sugar content that produces a better taste. However, when man subverts the maturing process, the anticipated mouth-watering flavor is not achieved.

The fifteenth chapter of John teaches us that only by abiding in the vine (Jesus) can our lives bring forth much fruit. All essential nutrients are supplied to us through the vine until we are completely "Son-ripened" and ready to enter His eternal harvest.

And here's a bonus. **Psalm 92** promises that "those who are planted in the house of the Lord shall flourish, and they shall bring forth fruit in old age."

Matthew 23: records the seven woes Jesus pronounced upon the Pharisees. Verse: 28 states, "Even so ye also outwardly appear righteous unto men, but within ye are full of hypocrisy and iniquity." Clearly, these Pharisees had not been through the process of Son-ripening.

Yes, it's true, "they just don't make tomatoes like they used to." But, it is also true that God's process of producing saints remains the same.

Abide in Him moment by moment, stay connected to the True Vine, and don't attempt to subvert His ripening process.

GEE, I SURE HOPE I PASSED THE TEST

Everyone settled into the Saturday morning class after a time of greeting one another. It was a comfortable atmosphere where over-age-fifty drivers had come to take the AARP Driver Safety Program course.

After passing a test, a certificate would be given which guaranteed a reduction in automobile insurance. Understandably, this was attractive to all of us.

The instructor was a genteel elderly man who enjoyed teaching the same course he had taught for years. He even read most of the 100 manual to the class.

We enjoyed his sense of humor; however, looks were exchanged and eyeballs rolled when he would read only lines one, three, and five of a paragraph omitting lines two and four altogether without even noticing.

Wearied from five hours of instruction, we completed our open-book test while he called out the answers. We were all past ready to get the certificate and go. At this point, jotting down his answers seemed much easier than searching through a hundred pages.

At the conclusion, he told us that the three leading vision problems of glaucoma, cataracts, and detached retinas were the main causes for elderly people ceasing to drive. This information was quickly followed by him saying, "But don't worry. I've got all three, and I'm still driving." I believe most of the class, like me, was thinking, "Gee, I sure hope I passed the test."

Our lives are lived as though we're taking an "open book test." Understanding God's word is essential. Being in relationship to Him while endeavoring to hear and heed His voice is what prepares us for eternity. There are many voices and many teachers giving much instruction. Make it your goal to discern the voice of God and to follow Him.

- ❖ **Proverbs 19:27** Cease, my son, to hear the instruction that causeth thee to err from the words of knowledge.
- ❖ **Proverbs 23:12** Apply thine heart unto instruction, and thine ears to the words of knowledge.

Walking in the truths mentioned in these two scriptures alone cannot be accomplished without a considerable amount of continual effort. Be assured that God sees your love and devotion to Him and that He will empower you to be successful.

Remember the words written by Luke concerning the Bereans:

Acts 17:11 ...they received the word with all readiness of mind, and searched the scriptures daily, whether those things were so.

While taking your life's "open-book test," finding God's answers by searching scripture is far better than jotting down answers from others. Earnestly pray while taking your "open-book test" knowing that your eternal destiny depends on your identifying what voice is speaking to you and whether or not you choose to follow.

Remember that just as **Philippians 2:12** warns, you are to "work out your own salvation with fear and trembling."

GIVE IT A FEW DAYS,
AND IT'LL ALL WORK OUT

Struggling through the consequences of an unusually rough divorce, Sherry would sometimes seek the counsel of a trusted friend. He was a refined older man who was also a Christian and an attorney.

Mr. Gaudin, known for being a patient listener, offered wise counsel, too. When he did speak, it was in fatherly tones. He never hurried anyone who was sharing their distressing burdens with him.

Sherry reflected on his counsel while driving home from one such meeting. She had described a no-win situation that had to be resolved within a short time. She could see no way out of this predicament. Then it dawned on her that Mr. Gaudin had given the same advice previously. As a matter of fact, a quick search of her memory bank provided a clearer picture.

She concluded, "Give it a few days, and it'll all work out," must be his standard advice, as she chuckled at the revelation. Another revelation brought another chuckle. His counsel had always been correct.
Sherry called Mr. Gaudin as soon as she arrived home. "I just want you to know you are going to have to give it up," was the remark she made following his welcoming, "Hello." Her statement puzzled him until she added, "I'm onto you now. I figured out that you always give the same advice, 'Give it a few days, and it'll all work out.'"

They then felt the warmth of a client and attorney who had become friends while Mr. Gaudin offered this explanation. He said that he had learned years ago that, in many instances, his clients would become distraught over situations that just needed a little time. In the interim, they needed someone who would listen.

Before long, Sherry was deeply distressed again. Only this time, she sought the counsel of the Lord in prayer. Bowing her head in anguished prayer while sitting at her kitchen table, she poured out her complaint. "God, you know that I love you. I try to tell people about you but no one will listen." Refreshing and pure like the morning dew, the Lord rebounded, "I'll listen." How precious and endearing was His answer.

His counsel did not come as, "Give it a few days, and it will all work out," but He led her gently day by day in the path He had ordained. With her hand in His, she looked to Him for the direction needed. And, true to His word, she found her Savior always listening to her every care and concern.

Sherry's heart was comforted when she thought of psalms written thousands of years ago:
    Psalm 3:4 I cried unto the Lord with my voice, and He heard me out of His holy hill.
    Psalm 116:1-2 I love the Lord, because he hath heard my voice and my supplications. Because he hath inclined his ear unto me, therefore will I call upon him as long as I live.

GOD OF THE RIBBONS

Just as casually as I asked, He casually answered. I had been dusting the furniture in my daughter Susie's bedroom while she was at school. As the mother of a precious nine-year-old, I had tried to stay tuned to her needs - even unspoken ones. However, I had no way of knowing if any need had been overlooked. No way, that is, other than asking the Lord God Almighty.

So, I prayed as I dusted, "Lord, is there anything she needs that I'm not aware of?" In an instant, the Spirit simply said, "Ribbons." Puzzled, I asked, "Ribbons? Do You mean 'hair ribbons?" Then I remembered seeing girls at her school wearing ribbons in their hair. I put away my cleaning materials and drove to a fabric store where I bought almost every color ribbon.

When Susie arrived home and walked into her room, she was literally overjoyed to see such an array of colorful ribbons laid across her bed. She danced while trying to decide which color would go best with her school clothes.

Hair ribbon is such a small thing and yet God was aware of the unspoken desire in a young girl's heart and graciously told me about it. How sensitive is our God! He is totally aware and totally loving. (And I was grateful that the desire of her heart could be so easily met).

I shared this unusual answer to prayer with Susie some years later. We have since prayed to the "God of the ribbons," many times having full confidence that He was aware and willing to meet any need we brought before Him.

If you think God is t-o-o big to be concerned with your small needs, try Him and see. Any matter of importance to you is important to Him. Answered prayers build a tremendous bond between the believer and the Creator.

Even today, decades later, Susie and I are still praying to the "God of the ribbons," and He has not failed or disappointed us.

GUESS I'LL READ IT AGAIN

Beth was troubled. Actually, she was deeply troubled and questioning why, after she had done her best to be an obedient and submissive wife, her husband, George, continued in a relentless, angry drunken tirade vehemently rejecting both God and her.

Beth had faithfully followed all the one-size-fits-all steps prescribed in seminars and sermons. Even though the guaranteed results never materialized, she continued to doggedly demonstrate a high level of perseverance while being misled by teaching based on misapplication of scripture. Her mind became a swamp of tainted beliefs.

One flawed teaching she adhered to was something like a "cause and effect" method of accomplishing goals in prayer. In other words, the message conveyed by certain Christian teachers was, "If you do this, God will do that." Somehow, a submissive attitude would compel God to move. However, it didn't, and He didn't.

She began frequent fasting hoping that if God wasn't moving, surely her fasting would move God. It didn't. In fact, the more she fasted, the more hostile George became as evil forces jockeyed to conquer his soul.

Since her thoroughly demonized husband could not tolerate the presence of a Bible, she kept hers out of sight in a laundry room cabinet. One day, however, while George was reclining in a den chair, Beth summonsed the courage to gather her Bible and walk within five feet of him on her way to a hoped for time of solitude in the bedroom.

She saw him notice the Bible held snugly to her heart as she glanced in his direction. His body was now ridged. He held his head back in the chair while clinching his teeth and rocking back and forth making guttural sounds. His nostrils flared. His face, neck, and arms were crimson red and dotted with white splotches. Some of the splotches were the size of quarters. It was evident that the battle to conquer his soul was raging in full-force.

Then, in absolute despair and without so much as offering a salutation, she blurted a silent prayer pleading, "Why does your word have so little to say to wives of unsaved husbands when it's such a prevalent problem?" Then, as bluntly as the question was blurted, the Lord retorted, "My word is complete!" Feeling the jolt of His displeasure, this wilted reply came from her lips, "I guess I'll read it again."

Beth did "read it again," and again and again. She continued failing to separate the personality from the principality. She simply lacked the wisdom and strength to deal with the evil power energizing her husband.

Another decade was to pass before George divorced her claiming she was a religious fanatic. During a seven hour divorce hearing, a number of false witnesses testified against her. God-called true witnesses testified of her sincerity. The judge ruled entirely in her favor.

God has lovingly continued His work of sanctification in Beth's life. Today she enjoys a blessed, fulfilling life and marriage to a loving, affectionate, and gentle soft-spoken Christan man.

Her former-husband's mind has deteriorated to the point of him being unreachable. He resides in a nursing home where he is subdued by anti-psychotic drugs.

Beth wonders when she recalls her former-husband's drunken outbursts threatening to put her in an insane asylum because of her love for God.

... having loved this present world ...

"... having loved this present world..." is a portion of a scripture passage from **2nd Timothy 4:10** where the Apostle Paul writes of being forsaken by Demas.

The complete scripture reads:
2nd Timothy 4:10 For Demas hath forsaken me, having loved this present world, and is departed unto Thessalonica.

This is the last mention of a man who had been with the Apostle Paul during his first and second imprisonments in Rome.

Earlier in **2nd Timothy 3:1-2**, Paul had written these words "... for men shall be lovers ..." Yes, men will be lovers - that is lovers of things not approved of God. These familiar scriptures list nineteen things that men prefer to love rather than God. And how heartbroken is our God?

Let's view the temporal world that Demas loved and chose over eternal bliss in the presence of God. For thousands of years, the Jews had been subjects of foreign rule including; Egyptian, Syrian, Babylonian, Persian, Greek, and Roman.

During Demas' time on earth, the Jews were unwilling subjects of Rome which ruled them through Herod, the Jewish-by-birth king who had been appointed by the Roman Emperor Julius Caesar.

Thessalonica was a city in Macedonia. It is presently the second largest city in Northern Greece. Paul had great success establishing a Jewish-Gentile church there after preaching at least three weeks in its synagogue.

Housing generally consisted of a one or two room square structure with a dirt floor, narrow doorways, and a wooden front door. People owned few personal items, slept on mats, wore simple clothing and sandals. Water was carried from a local well and oil lamps were used for lighting. Obviously, what would be termed as a "modern-day convenience" or of what today's revelers would refer to as "the good life" was thousands of years in the future.

From what is known of the living conditions and political climate of Demas' day, we can only wonder what enticement Satan used to ensnare his soul. Whatever the attraction was, it caused him to waltz right off the Holy pages and into oblivion.

God's word admonishes us not to love the world.

1st John 2:15-17 Love not the world, neither the things that be of the world. If any man love the world, the love of the Father is not in him. For all that is of the world, the lust of the flesh, and the lusts of the eyes, and the pride of life, is not of the Father, but is of the world. And the world passeth away, and the lusts thereof: but he that doeth the will of God abideth forever.

HE IS ABLE

Here is a list of scriptures that tell us what our God is able to do.

Daniel 3:17 ... our God, whom we serve, **is able** to deliver us from the burning fiery furnace...

Matthew 3:9 ... **God is able** of these stones to raise up children unto Abraham.

2nd Corinthians 9:8 And **God is able** to make all grace abound toward you, that ye, always having all sufficiency in all things, may abound to every good work.

Ephesians 3:20-21 Now unto **him who is able** to do exceedingly abundantly above all that we ask or think, according to the power that worketh in us, unto him be glory in the church by Christ Jesus throughout all ages, world without end. Amen.

Philippians 3:21 ... **he is able** even to subdue all things unto himself.

2nd Timothy 1:12 ... for I know whom I have believed and am persuaded that **he is able** to keep that which I have committed unto him against that day.

Hebrews 2:18 For in that he himself hath suffered being tempted, **he is able** to help them that are tempted.

Hebrews 7:25 Wherefore, **he is able** also to save them to the uttermost that come unto God by him, seeing he ever liveth to make intercession for them.

Jude :24-25 Now unto him that **is able** to keep you from falling, and to present you faultless before the presence of his glory with exceeding joy, to the only wise God, our Savior, be glory and majesty, dominion and power, both now and ever. Amen.

Knowing the things that He is able to do is wonderful. Knowing He is doing them for you is awesome. Thoughts of what He plans to do in your future are overwhelmingly delightful. Purpose in your heart to meditate on who He is throughout the day, and remember the words written by **Isaiah 26:3** which say, "Thou wilt keep him in perfect peace, whose mind is stayed upon thee.

HE NOTICES HOW WE GIVE

Brother Roy Smith was a discouraged elderly man who had been crippled by arthritis. You couldn't help but notice how difficult it was for him to enter church, walk down the center aisle, and take a seat alongside his sister. Though his body was stooped, he always looked up with a bright smile for all that greeted him.

The acute pain of arthritis was not the only chronic pain Brother Roy felt. Years that should have been productive were taken away by his inability to work or to live independently. His feeling of uselessness increased as he aged.

He received a call from a relative living in Arkansas asking him to come and live with him and his family. Brother Roy agreed thinking maybe this was God making a way for him to reach these unchurched family members.

He hadn't been in Arkansas long when I received a letter from him in which he had included his tithe. He had decided to continue giving our church his tithe until he found a suitable church. Looking back, I am sure it was the Lord who prompted me to write thanking him for doing so. Each month thereafter, Brother Roy sent his tithe, and I would send an acknowledgment letter and fill him in on our church's news.

Then another Holy Ghost inspired thought came into my heart. I wrote him a letter to let him know that his tithes had been used to purchase the entire third quarter Junior High Sunday School curriculum and to thank him for sending it.

Little did anyone know that he would return shortly to our church. He would enter the same door, walk the same center aisle, and sit in the same seat next to his sister. He was a different man now. Roy radiated a glow unseen before.

What had made the difference? It was knowing that his tithe was not just a drop in the bucket, that it had been put to good use, and that his faithful giving was recognized and appreciated.

Brother Roy came to me and said he would gladly give more if the church needed it. Knowing his gift would be a sacrifice, I thanked him and assured him I would let him know should a need arise.

Mark 12:41-44 tells of an occasion that actually happened. It is not a parable. Jesus sat opposite the temple treasury and beheld <u>how</u> the people gave. He's still doing that today. He noticed many rich casting in much. He saw a poor widow casting in two mites that make a farthing the smallest coinage measurement. Then He declared that the poor widow had cast in more than the rich, because she had cast in all she had. Obviously, He's aware of those who give their all.

Brother Roy had given his all and was willing to give more. Jesus had noticed <u>how</u> he gave with a willing heart. Brother Roy has gone on to the glory world but the knowledge of God imparted to the Junior High Sunday School through his faithful giving is still producing life in those youngsters. Some may have seen Brother Roy as a crippled elderly man who had nothing to contribute to the Kingdom. But God noticed <u>how</u> he gave and knew that his giving was a sacrifice. Actually, he may have given more than wealthy church members.

1st Corinthians 4:5 warns us to judge nothing before the Lord comes and judges man's deeds. It says, "(the Lord) will make manifest the counsels of the hearts; and then shall every man have praise of God."

HE WARNED THE STRANGER

Randall Landry was never one to mince words. Though never rude, he addressed situations in a straight forward manner. God used that trait to deliver a timely message to the stranger.

Randall was in the church's sound booth making adjustments prior to the start of the Sunday evening service. That's when he noticed the stranger enter the sanctuary.

Having an unknown visitor wasn't that uncommon, but there was something different about this man. He took a seat near the front as members continued welcoming the stranger. Following an invigorating worship service, the pastor began his message.

Randall continued observing the stranger. Though seeing only the man's back, he could perceive something was terribly wrong. He asked God to show him what it was.

The pastor sensed that God was changing his message and that He wanted it to go in a direction he hadn't anticipated. He began giving a strong exhortation for those listening "to get it right with God." His anointed message pleaded for total surrender.

By this time, God had placed a tremendous burden on Randall for the stranger's soul. Obeying the unction of God, he left the sound booth and walked directly to where the stranger was seated. He knelt by his side in the aisle and spoke these words given directly by the Lord, "You have been called many times, and you have refused. The call you hear tonight will be your last. If you choose not to respond, you will doom your soul." The stranger stiffened, as his heart remained callous and impenitent.

The pastor concluded the message and issued an altar call. Others responded; the stranger did not. Randall shook his head as he saw the stranger walk out of the sanctuary and into the vestibule. Thinking that maybe a final word might persuade him to reconsider, he approached the stranger again. This final attempt also failed. Randall returned to the sound booth to shut the system down. The screeching sounds of an 18-wheeler's air breaks and metal being mangled with metal were unmistakable. He ran out the front door dreading to see what he knew he would see.

An 18-wheeler had creamed the stranger's truck as it pulled out of the church's parking lot onto the state highway. The stranger's life was tragically ended.

- ❖ **2nd Corinthians 5:11** Knowing, therefore, the terror of the Lord, we persuade men..."

- ❖ **Hebrews 10:31** It is a fearful thing to fall into the hands of the living God.

HELLO, MY NAME IS VIRGINIA LAWRENCE

"Hello, my name is Virginia Lawrence, and I'm new in town," was the cheerful greeting she spoke as she entered Greenburg's only nursing home. The receptionist looked up into the joyful face of a woman who lived a life devoted to the good of others. She was to repeat her self-introduction later that day in a small hospital located near her new-found church.

Virginia Lawrence was then an amiable eighty-four-year-old widow who had walked melodiously with Jesus throughout her lifetime. When her son and daughter-in-law announced they had purchased a lovely home in the country surrounded by pine forests, low sloping hills, and countless azaleas, she enthusiastically anticipated seeing it for herself.

She mulled over in her mind Bill and Libby's offer of her making her home with them. Their offer seemed more like gentle insistence, and Virginia realized that no longer living alone may be in her best interest. Her Savior had taught her to be willing to adjust and go on.

As they drove through the countryside, she observed that it was actually more beautiful than she had envisioned as her eyes soaked in its beauty. Little did she know that her new hometown would embrace her as a dollop of God's love and kindness.

However, the adjustments required were more than she expected. Much to her disappointment, she found that the kitchen in her spacious new home would not become her prized domain. She discovered, too, that her own private space had been relegated to a bedroom at the end of the hall. Sighing deeply, she relinquished both. Virginia was tempted to allow the made-for-her decisions to dampen her spirit. While in prayer, she determined that **Romans 8:28** was still true. These well-loved and often quoted words guarantee the believer, "…that all things work together for good to them that love God, to them who are the called according to his purpose." She remained tranquil knowing He was changing the season in her life.

Virginia resolved to do what believers are directed to do in **James 1:27**, which says, "Pure religion and undefiled before God and the Father is this: to visit the fatherless and widows in their affliction, and to keep oneself unspotted from the world."

Obeying this one scripture caused her to present herself as a volunteer who wanted to visit the residents of the nursing home and the hospital's patients soon. Both facilities knew she was just what was needed to lift others from the doldrums.

Virginia began visiting twice a week to whomever the staffs recommended. Her visits were always welcomed. Her experience was true to Jesus' word which says it is more blessed to give than to receive. She reaped as much benefit as those she visited.

Her church supplied a list of elderly home-bound members. Though elderly herself, she began visiting them also. Their spirits were buoyed by her attention and gracious warmth. Each visit was preceded by a phone call pledging, "I am not going to eat your food. I am bringing you some fresh fruit. I won't stay long. We will talk of the Lord and share our hearts in prayer."

One summer morning, while John and Libby were away, Virginia heard an unidentified sound coming from the hallway. As she emerged from her bedroom whispering a prayer, she encountered a frightening looking woman who had made her entrance through a bathroom window. Energized from above, Virginia fearlessly demanded, "What are you doing in my home?" The intruder stammered a drug drenched response. Virginia then directed her to a kitchen chair where she could sit while awaiting the police.

A call to the sheriff's office brought two police officers within minutes. The officers were well acquainted with the burglar. She was the sheriff's daughter. No charges were filed as no real harm had been done. With her focus on Jesus, sober-minded Virginia had remained composed and undisturbed. (The sheriff admitted his daughter to a medical facility equipped to help in such situations).

Virginia continued her ministry of caring for others until a few weeks before her homecoming on May 16, 2002.

Not everyone adapts well to changes that propel them into an unknown zone in the evening of their lifetime. But Virginia had been made ready by learning to walk with Jesus day-by-day while expecting Him to create opportunities to show His love to others along the way.

Just as the Apostle Paul admonished in **Ephesians 4:1**, "I therefore, the prisoner of the Lord, beseech you that ye walk worthy of the vocation to which you are called."

Truly, Virginia Lawrence walked worthy of the vocation to which she was called.

HER HEART WAS BURSTING

The Lord started telling me about Sue as I was driving home. He engaged my heart to feel her intense burden. Her heart was wrenched and snarled with immobilizing pain. The Lord said that her heart was bursting and just couldn't hold any more. The weight of her struggle was placed upon me. I knew I had to pray and touch God for her. I hurried onto my house anticipating what God was going to do.

When I reached her on the phone and heard the sound of her sparkling voice, I carefully said, "Sue, I wanted to tell you that I'm getting ready to pray, and your name is at the top of my list." She burst into squalls, and I waited. Then there was silence. As she was able to regain her composure, she said, "Gladys, the Lord told me that you would call and that you would pray."

We plunged immediately into a battle royal prayer. The anointing of God was more than enough to defeat the forces of darkness plaguing her. We were both aware the moment the power of Satan was dispelled in Jesus name. I never knew what I was praying about, but I didn't need to know.

Satan would like the world to see him as a cartoon caricature and not as the "little g" God of this world. The amount of misery he inflicts daily is unknown by us but surely not unknown unto God. One of his strategies is to wound believers and work to isolate them from others who could and would come to their aid.

Fortunately, Sue had cried out to God for deliverance. He responded by laying her burden on me. Then, He gave the power to defeat Satan in prayer. This is the way He desires the body of Christ to function. What a mighty God we serve!

HONOR THE LORD WITH THY SUBSTANCE

Noticing tread-worn tires must be a "man-thing." Warning someone that their car tires lacked sufficient tread must also be considered a "man-thing."

As Roger walked by and saw a woman getting out of her car, he commented to her on the dangerous condition of her tires. With a wave of her hand and with shoulders shrugged, she dismissed his concern with, "Oh, my sweet Jesus will take care of my tires!" The observer quickly added, "Lady, if I were you, I wouldn't push 'My sweet Jesus too far.'

This woman may have been influenced by the erroneous teaching that a Christian is to "have faith in your faith." Unfortunately, many latched onto this teaching without a careful examination of the Word of God. Luke recorded in **Acts 17:11** that the noble believers in Bere'a, "...received the word with all readiness of mind, and searched the scriptures daily, whether those things were so."

We are instructed in **Romans 10:17** that, "...faith cometh by hearing, and hearing by the word of God." It's our hearing from God that produces the faith to believe and to act.

It is sometimes emphasized that Elijah acted after seeing the little cloud "like a man's hand." However, true to God's word, Elijah's faith came by hearing. **1st Kings 18:41** states that Elijah first of all "heard the sound of abundance of rain." His faith to speak and act came by hearing.

Scripture further teaches believers that "faith is the substance of things hoped for, the evidence of things not seen. **(Hebrews 11:1)**

Proverbs 3:9 Honor the Lord with thy substance...

Let's view "faith" as our "sub-stance." Imagine a soldier standing at attention with his weapon by his side. In this posture, he actually could be easily knocked over. Imagine him again holding his weapon and standing in a rigid position with his right leg braced in strength, left leg extended with knee bent forward, and his weapon aimed. In this stance, he is more able to defeat his enemy.

Having a true "sub-stance" that honors God means that you have heard from Him and you are prepared to act and speak accordingly.

Was the woman with the tread-less tires acting on God-given faith or was she coasting down the road of life on presumption or self-generated faith? Was she honoring God with her sub-stance?

The gospels of Matthew and Mark record that Jesus said, "...the Son of man came not to be ministered unto, but to minister..." And, yet, in **Luke 8:2-3**, we are told that certain women, including Mary Magdalene, Joanna, Susanna, and many others, "ministered unto Him of their substance."

Not all believers are ministering unto Him with their <u>substance</u> or true faith that comes from hearing God's voice. Endeavor to make it your life's goal to hear and heed His voice. You won't regret the time spent listening for the voice of your Savior.

I DON'T THINK I COULD ADD A THING...

Mourners shuffled back and forth in the funeral home's parlor and could be heard lamenting the loss of their friend at such an early age. Bobby Jenkins had only lived twenty-eight years when tragically killed in a boating accident leaving a young wife and two small sons to mourn his loss.

His unexpected death left his family and friends grief stricken and unprepared. As was his custom in such circumstance, the funeral director suggested Brother Jones, a retired minister, be called to conduct the funeral service.

Brother Jones was happy to be of assistance and dutifully arrived well ahead of the scheduled service time hoping to learn details of Bobby's life to aid him in offering words of comfort.

He meandered through the crowd hoping to glean from their conversations. Brother Jones was dismayed to hear the comments of this young man's life lived in the fast lane. Thinking he would just make the best of the situation, he stood by the open coffin and waited for the time to begin the service.

That's when he noticed the relics placed alongside Bobby in his coffin; a box of Skoal Chewing Tobacco and a six pack of Bud Light beer. Alarmed at seeing these, his mind began to race knowing the service time was minutes away, and he still had no words of comfort or condolence.

Brother Jones felt relief when two young men, a cousin and a companion of the deceased, asked if they could speak and "testify" of the departed man's life. The request encouraged Brother Jones and he thought that maybe, just maybe, there had been some noteworthy merit exhibited by this man before his death.

However, that was not to be. Brother Jones stood by the coffin and managed to maintain his composure as buddy after buddy came forward to "testify" of what a tremendous party animal Bobby Jenkins had been; "Why, he could drink for days and never pass out. Come Friday, he had plenty of money with which to treat his friends to a good time. He lived his life to the fullest, and never ran out of jokes to entertain his laughing fans," were some of the boastful comments.

Brother Jones, speaking with all the dignity he could muster, stepped to the microphone and concluded the service by saying, "I don't think I could add a thing to what's already been said."

My friend, at this point, all had been said and all had been done. Bobby Jenkins had lived his short life and never learned of the BIBLE.

- **Basic Instruction Before Leaving Earth**
- **Hebrews 9:27** ... it is appointed unto men once to die, but after this the judgment.

Three of the gospels quote Jesus as asking, "For what shall it profit a man, if he shall gain the whole world, and lose his own soul?"

I WAS JUST GONNA SMELL IT, LORD

Allen Taylor, who is known to most everyone as "Pa Allen," has decades of memories of how God has brought him through life's maze.

When much of his youth had been obliterated by his indulgence in booze, he turned to God for deliverance. Our great God then delivered him and began an astonishing work of restoration in Pa Allen. He became the jovial husband and father that he had longed to be deep within the crevasses of his heart. In the ensuing years, with the help of God, Pa Allen was to remain faithful to the promise of sobriety he had made to God. He walked in victory feeling the immense satisfaction of an overcomer.

In his declining years, Pa Allen discovered a carefully laid snare which he came upon in an unsuspecting moment. He had gone out to his shop behind his home to begin the arduous task of cleaning out a lifetime of debris. He was enjoying the effects of a cool breeze coming through opened doors at each end of his large shop. He stooped to scoop some rubbish piled around a post when he spied a half empty bottle of booze waiting and just within reach. With his memory sensors already serenaded, he picked up the bottle and removed its lid. Simultaneously, an enormous lightning bolt struck the ground just outside illuminating his entire shop, as he lifted the open bottle. The force of that one bolt rattled more than the walls around Pa Allen. His knees knocked together as cymbals and his voice quivered as he threw the bottle down shouting, "I was just gonna smell it, Lord!" God, by a thunder clap and a lightning bolt, had sovereignly delivered him from what could have catapulted him back onto the path of destruction.

In the very beginning chapter of Genesis, God gave man dominion over the things on earth and told him to subdue it. However, some of the things growing out of the earth have subdued and conquered man.

Weeds, called marijuana, subdue and conquer man. Poppy seeds, processed into opium, subdue and conquer man. Man makes alcohol from corn and barley. And who could determine the amount of human misery derived from the cocaine producing Coca plant? Instead of subduing the earth, these small and insignificant weeds, seeds, and plants have subdued and conquered many a man. What a sad commentary.

The bottle of booze was a snare put in place years before to tempt him with just one glimpse followed by just one sniff. Bondage to sin always takes us further than we want to go and keeps us longer than we want to stay.

Pa Allen had received a dose of the fear of the Lord sufficient enough to deliver him. **Proverbs 16:6** affirms, "…by the fear of the Lord men depart from evil." God used Pa Allen's "fear of the Lord" to make a way of escape for him. As the Apostle Paul informed the saints at Corinth, "There hath no temptation taken you but such as is common to man; but God is faithful, who will not permit you to be tempted above that ye are able, but will, with the temptation, also make a way to escape, that ye may be able to bear it." **(1st Corinthians 10:13)**

Proverbs 1:17 assures us, "Surely in vain the net is spread in the sight of any bird."

Those who walk circumspectly are given keen peripheral vision like birds. They are ever-alert to the circumstances around them. Those who call upon the way-maker God in truth are able to escape the snare of Satan.

IF BRENDA COULD TALK TO YOU NOW

It had been said figuratively that Brenda was born on a bar stool, lived on a bar stool, and died on a bar stool. Her death was not unexpected when cancer took her life at age fifty.

What was unexpected was her daughter's insistence that the family's pastor present his funeral message as though Brenda had lived a life acceptable to God. This type of request is not all that uncommon. In fact, being asked to "preach momma (or whoever) saved," when there is no evidence of Biblical salvation, is sometimes more of a demand than a request.

Pastor Robertson understood the family's grief and disappointment. The message he presented provided comfort to Brenda's mourners without robbing them of their fragile belief in her salvation. He trusted that in the ensuing years the knowledge of true Biblical salvation would be working its way into their hearts. His duty, as pastor, was to offer comfort without compromise to the mourners.

His carefully chosen words included statements like; "Brenda has passed on to the other side. If she could talk to you now, she would want you all to know how important it is to love God." These words of truth peacefully settled their emotions as Pastor Robertson continued, "She would tell you that once your life has ended you won't have another opportunity to choose to serve God. She certainly would want you to live lives acceptable to Him. Brenda would not want any of you to miss out on entering the glory world to be with Jesus."

His comments had actually been derived from the following scriptures:

2nd Corinthians 5:9-11 Wherefore, we labor that, whether present or absent, we may be accepted of Him. For we must all appear before the judgment seat of Christ, that everyone may receive the things done in his body according to that which he hath done, whether good or bad. Knowing, therefore the terror of the Lord, we persuade men...

1st Corinthians 2:9 But it is written, Eye hath not seen, nor ear heard, neither have entered into the heart of man, the things which God hath prepared for them that love Him.

Our Lord's half-brother penned the following strong exhortation recorded in **James 4:13-14**, "Come now, ye that say, Today or tomorrow we will go into such a city, and continue there a year, and buy and sell, and get gain; Whereas ye know not what shall be on the morrow. For what is your life? It is even a vapor that appears for a little time, and then vanishes away."

One of the earliest written psalms is Psalm 90. It is a prayer of Moses which he wrote and sung thousands of years ago. In it, he pleaded with God, "So teach us to number our days, that we may apply our hearts unto wisdom."

Brenda, like countless others, has no more days to number. However, if you are reading these words, then you are alive and have opportunity to love God and to live for His glory.

Please don't let this moment pass from your grasp. When you begin speaking to Him and listening for His voice, He will manifest Himself to you personally in ways you never thought possible.

IF THE LORD BE WITH US

One of the most interesting questions asked in the Bible is found in **Judges 6:13** where we find Gideon responding to the angel of the Lord who had appeared and sat under an oak tree while saying, "The Lord is with *thee,* thou mighty man of valor." Gideon then asked, "O, my Lord, if the Lord be with us, why then is all this befallen us? And where are all His miracles which our fathers told us of ..."

Gideon belonged to the tribe of Manasseh that occupied the Plain of Esdraelon, the place where Armageddon will be fought. Notice that God's "mighty man of valor" was threshing wheat by the wine press in order to hide it from the enemy.

The Midianites, like the Amalekites, were a nomadic disorganized tribe. They conquered whomever and whatever they encountered. Through fear of them, the children of Israel had fled to the hills to live in caves leaving their crops for the enemy to devour.

BUT God had appointed Gideon as a deliverer. Under His direction, Gideon was to become the sixth judge and the first judge whose history would be narrated. During his rule, God's people would enjoy forty years of peace.

Remember that the Lord's angel had told him, "The Lord is with **thee** ..." And his response was, "**if** the Lord be with **us**, why then is all this befallen **us**?"

Knowing the pitiful backslidden condition of Israel, why would Gideon ask such a question? The truth of the matter was that God was with Gideon and desired to use him with three hundred untrained, unarmed soldiers to defeat the skilled 120,000 man Midianite army for His glory.

Read the entire account and you will find that God never gave Gideon direct answers to his questions. He merely used Him for His purpose. You, too, will have unanswered questions while on this side of the glory world.

Part of God's purpose was to demonstrate to His beloved-Israel that they were His people and that He would fight their battles and defeat those who opposed them.

Can feeble fallen finite man require the Creator of ALL things seen and unseen to give an account for what He chooses? God may not always give us clear understanding of all He determines best. He does, however, give us abundant grace and mercy for each obstacle we encounter.

Gideon was aware of being in a treacherous and overwhelming situation with no way out. He was not aware of the victory God had chosen to bring about or the forthcoming forty years of peace He planned to bestow.

And neither can we see all that He is bringing about in our lives. We see only the magnitude of the battle without seeing the magnitude of the triumph. We can, however, trust Him to work everything for our good and according to His purpose.

IT WAS A MAN IN A BUSINESS SUIT

Even years ago it wasn't wise for a woman to be driving alone at night on an Interstate highway over our inner-city areas known to have crime problems. However, this was what I found myself doing as I drove home around 10:00 p.m. after a church service in the northern part of our parish. I was alone yet not alone knowing my Savior was with me.

Still feeling a little uneasy, I became more aware of the flow of traffic which was pretty heavy for late on a Friday night. I started to wonder how many of the drivers had been drinking. I was in the far-left lane of the three-lane interstate driving next to a concrete wall. There in my lane was what looked like a metal grill.

I glanced to the right. There were too many vehicles all coming too fast for me to make a lane change. The concrete wall to my left wasn't an option. I looked ahead at the grill, held both hands on the steering wheel, and braced for better control. POW! Hitting the grill made a loud sound I hadn't expected. The traffic in the other two lanes flowed by as I drifted over to the far right lane. Certain that my new back left tire was flat, I drifted off to the shoulder of the road just below an overpass.

Well, isn't this wonderful, I thought. Here I am at 10:00 p.m. Friday stuck on the side of the Interstate with a flat tire in a bad area of town. (This happened years before the cell phone was invented). I comforted myself by acknowledging to God that He knew I was there and that I wasn't alone. Surely this was no problem for God, right?

I decided to count to one hundred and by then God would send someone to help me. I began counting and dragged out the last 90-91-92... Okay, it didn't work. I'll just go on to Plan B. Another thought came into focus: God would protect me if I stood by the trunk of my car to emphasize my helplessness. As I walked to the back of the car, I asked God to send a policeman to help me. I was thinking that there might be a policeman out patrolling for drunk drivers. Many vehicles whizzed by but not one stopped or even slowed.

All right, it was time to get serious. Oh, good, an even better thought permeated my mind. I would ask God to send a man in a business suit to help my helplessness. I considered this to be a brilliant request since He hadn't sent a policeman, and I might not trust an ordinary looking man. Yes, I am woman, and, yes, such thinking can seem reasonable to a woman in distress. So I asked God to send a man in a business suit.

My attention turned to the top of the overpass I had drifted down. Lo and behold, there was a car stopping by an abandoned car. A man got out of the car and walked all the way around the abandoned car. The Interstate was well lighted, and I thought, "Just look at that man. He's checking out an abandoned car. Can't he see that car is abandoned? I'm the one down here not going anywhere."

As I looked, I saw him begin to walk toward me. Well, at least he has on a business suit, I thought. I noticed him holding something in his outstretched hand and coming toward yours truly. The man in the business suit was showing his policeman's badge so I wouldn't be afraid!

In response to my prayer, my God had sent an undercover agent dressed in a business suit at 10:00 p.m. to change my tire on the Interstate!

IT'S MORE THAN AN IDEAL FUNERAL MESSAGE

Even un-churched people are familiar with the verses found in **John 14:1-4** since ministers often use these verses to comfort mourners at funerals.

John 14:1-4 Let not your heart be troubled; ye believe in God, believe also in me. In my Father's house are many mansions; if it were not so, I would have told you. I go to prepare a place for you. And if I go and prepare a place for you, I will come again, and receive you unto myself, that where I am, there ye may be also. And where I go ye know, and the way ye know.

A closer look reveals that these words were never intended as an ideal funeral message. They are actually part of a private conversation between Jesus and Peter which began in John 13:37 and continued through 14:4. Casual half-conscience Bible reading will not detect that Chapter 14 is a continuance of the conversation Jesus begun in Chapter 13.

Their conversation went like this: (The name Peter is interjected to emphasize that Jesus was speaking alone to Peter).

John 13:37-38 <u>Peter</u> said unto Him, Lord, why cannot I follow thee now? I will lay down my life for thy sake. Jesus answered him (<u>Peter</u>). Wilt thou lay down thy life for my sake? <u>Verily, verily</u>, I say unto thee (<u>Peter</u>), The cock shall not crow, till thou hast denied me thrice. **14:1-2-4** Let not your heart (Peter) be troubled: ye believe in God, believe also in me. In my Father's house are many mansions; if it were not so, I would have told you (Peter.) I go to prepare a place for you (Peter.)And if I go and prepare a place for you (Peter,) I will come again, and receive you (Peter) unto myself, that where I am there ye (Peter) may be also. And where I go ye (Peter) know, and the way ye know.

Knowing full-well the soon-to-happen failures of Peter, the Good Shepherd was careful to assure him.

The Gospel of John records Jesus using the term "Verily, verily" fifty-two times and it is the only gospel that records its use. It simply means "truly or surely." Jesus knew that Peter would "truly or surely" deny Him three times, and He added, "Let not your heart be troubled..."
Later in the discourse recorded in Luke 22:31-32, just prior to His suffering, though filled with sorrow, Jesus again undergirds Peter. He spoke his name twice to gain his complete attention.

Verse :31-32 And the Lord said, Simon, Simon, behold, Satan hath desired to have you, that he may sift you as wheat. But I have prayed for thee, that thy faith fail not. And when thou art converted, strengthen thy brethren.

Notice that Jesus chose not to prevent this sifting of Peter. He knew that through His intercession Peter would survive the sifting or testing of Satan and that he would emerge a better and more fully equipped man.

The sifting separates the desirable wheat from the chaff or the unusable portion. In this metaphor, the wheat represents Peter and the chaff represents Peter's self-confidence or pride. Jesus knew that if the chaff remained it would be a great hindrance to Peter's accomplishing what God had appointed to accomplish through him.

Jesus didn't pray that Peter would not fail but that his faith in God would not fail. Jesus used the word, "converted," which is a Greek word (#1994) that simply means "turned about." The Book of Acts makes it abundantly clear that, when Peter was converted or turned about, he did indeed strengthen his brethren.

Matthew 27:3-4: Then, Judas who had betrayed Him, when he saw that He was condemned, <u>repented</u>, and brought again the thirty pieces of silver to the chief priests and elders, saying, I have sinned in that I have betrayed innocent blood.

Overwhelmed by guilt, Judas repented that he betrayed an innocent man. He hung himself without recognizing that the innocent man was the Son of God.

In direct contrast, **Matthew 26:75** states:
"And Peter remembered the words Jesus said unto him, before the cock crows twice thou shalt deny me thrice and he went out and wept bitterly. Peter knew he had done an unimaginable wrong; however he was sustained by the intercessory prayer of Jesus."

Hebrews 7:25 Wherefore, He is able also to save them to the uttermost that come unto God by Him, seeing He ever liveth to make intercession for them.

To better understand the written language of God and the ways He chooses to reveal Himself, we must carefully and prayerfully examine the word of God. For instance, it is not a coincidence that each of the three scriptures listing the names of the twelve disciples all list Peter first and Judas Iscariot last. This is God's thinly-veiled way of honoring one while dishonoring another.

Following His resurrection, the angel told the women at the tomb, **(Mark 16:7)** "But go your way, tell his disciples, and Peter, that He goeth before thee into Galilee..."

Surely this was done in order to reassure the heartsick Peter that he was still a disciple of the risen Lord and that all was well. How tenderly and carefully our Savior deals with His own.

The term, "fire of coals," is mentioned twice in the gospels and both relate to God's redemptive care of Peter. The first mention is in John 18:18 immediately following Peter's first of three denials which were all spoken while in the presence of Jesus.

John 18:18 And the servants and the officers stood there, who had made a fire of coals; for it was cold, and they warmed themselves; and Peter stood with them, and warmed himself.

Let's fast-forward to after the resurrection when Jesus appeared to seven of His disciples at the Sea of Tiberias (Sea of Galilee). The twenty-first chapter of John tells of Jesus appearing to the disciples in the morning after they had fished all night without catching any fish. He asked them, "Children, have ye any food? And they answered

Him, "No." He then tells them where to cast their net to find an abundance.

The fourth chapter of Matthew records the beginning of Jesus' public ministry when He called His first disciples, Peter and his brother Andrew. It is noteworthy that this occasion was also at the Sea of Galilee.

Matthew 4:18-20 And Jesus, walking by the Sea of Galilee, saw two brethren, Simon, called Peter, and Andrew, his brother, casting a net into the sea; for they were fishers. And He said unto them. Follow me, and I will make you fishers of men. And they straightway left their nets, and followed Him.

The association of these brothers with Jesus began as they were fishing by the Sea of Galilee. Now, after His resurrection, He comes to them again at the Sea of Tiberias (Galilee) as they are fishing. These events may seem unconnected; however, we will learn that being called into discipleship and later being restored into fellowship were essential and significant elements of Peter's future effectiveness for God. Jesus will skillfully use Peter's memory of his first encounter with Jesus as a healing tool. Here in the twenty-first chapter of John, after obeying the Lord's direction on where to cast their nets, they began to recognize that the One doing the directing was the Lord Himself. The still impetuous Peter then cast himself into the sea in an effort to reach Jesus. Could it be that he had a greater need to touch the risen Lord than the others?

John 21:9 As soon, then, as they were come to land, they saw a <u>fire of coals</u> there, and fish laid on it, and bread.

Notice how skillfully Jesus reconstructed the previous circumstance of a <u>fire of coals</u>. Surely, this scene was not significant to the other disciples. We can only imagine the tide of emotion surging through Peter's heart and mind as he observed Jesus at the <u>fire of coals</u>. This was a true "deja vu" experience for Peter.

This is the third time Jesus has appeared to His disciples following His resurrection. Just as Peter had uttered three denials, Jesus will restore him by providing three opportunities for him to affirmatively declare his love for Him.

Jesus invited them to "come and dine." He began speaking directly to Peter in verses :15-17:

John 21:15-16-17 So when they had dined, Jesus saith to Simon Peter, Simon, son of Jonah, lovest thou me more than these? He saith unto Him, Yea, Lord; thou knowest that I love thee. He saith unto him, Feed my lambs. He saith unto him again a second time, Simon, son of Jonah, lovest thou me? He saith unto him, Yea, Lord; thou knowest that I love thee. He saith unto him, Feed my sheep. He saith unto him the <u>third</u> time, Simon, son of Jonah, lovest thou me? Peter was grieved because He said unto him a third time, that I love thee. Jesus said unto him, Feed my sheep.

With this dramatic and necessary restoration, Peter became "converted" and made ready to "strengthen" his brethren. His name is mentioned fifty-six times in the book of The Acts of the Apostles. He, along with John, boldly proclaimed the truth before the Sanhedrin and others who knew "they were unlearned and ignorant men," and "they took knowledge of them, that they had been with Jesus." **(Acts 4:13)**

A listing of the events in Peter's ministry in The Acts of the Apostles includes: the healing of the born-lame man at Jerusalem, being twice cast into prison and both times being delivered by an angel, the healing of the man sick with palsy at Lydda, the raising of Dorcas from the dead at Joppa, and the bringing of the gospel to the Gentiles beginning with Cornelius the Roman centurion, his kinsmen and friends at Caesarea.

God knew the sifting of Peter was necessary to remove all possible hindrances to the ministry that He had ordained. Jesus knew that His intercessory prayer for Peter would strengthen him for the his ministry ahead.

Dear fellow pilgrim, rejoice in your walk with God even though He may allow a little sifting for your perfection.

IT'S NOT AS PRETTY AS HER HEART

Typically, prior to the opening prayer of the Sunday night church service, the pastor would say, "Take the hand of the person next to you, and let's pray together."

Kathy's only objections were that she didn't always know the persons next to her, and sometimes they would be left holding hands while the pastor made lengthy comments. Holding an unknown hand that begins to sweat in her own becoming-sweaty palm made her feel a little skirmish.

During one such service, when the pastor made the request, Kathy looked down and reached to the hand of an African-American woman seated next to her. Kathy noticed the smooth brown texture of the woman's forearm thinking that it resembled a bar of chocolate. She thought, "Oh, her arm is so pretty. I wish I could touch it." Our ever-listening Lord, then added, "It's not as pretty as her heart."

How did this woman with the pretty heart desire, achieve, and maintain such an accomplishment while living in a dark world of filled with sin-laden people?
Part of the answer is found in Ezekiel 36: an exhilarating chapter full of the "I will" declarations of God. Promises like; "A new heart also will I give you, and a new spirit will I put within you; and I will take away the stony heart out of your flesh, I will give you a heart of flesh, I will put my Spirit within you, I will save you from all your uncleanness, I will lay no famine upon you, and I the Lord have spoken it and I will do it."

Even a quick reading of this chapter is reassuring to those who know God can be relied upon to perform what He has promised. But don't read it too quickly while on your way for a fun day at the mall or ball park.

Read, meditate, and act upon His prerequisite found at the conclusion of the chapter in verse :37; "<u>Thus saith the Lord God, I will yet for this be inquired of by the house Israel, to do it for them</u>."

Without a doubt, the woman with the pretty heart had sought the Lord to continually cleanse her from the ever-present deluge of iniquity seeking to engulf the children of God. Surely, she could not live separate from the world and consecrated unto God without a deep desire to do so. In the seventh chapter of Zechariah, God pronounced judgment against those who have refused to hear His law and have made their hearts as an <u>adamant stone</u>. Adamant means an inflexible utterly unyielding attitude.

God's word makes a sharp contrast between "a heart of flesh," and "a heart of stone." The flesh of man is flexible and pliable and responds to touch. It is not at all like an unresponsive adamant stone.

This is written to encourage you not to neglect so great a salvation. So great that God the Father is willing to examine our hearts and to purge us from all hidden faults. And, yet, He must be inquired of to do it for us.

shall be judged by the law of liberty. For he shall have <u>judgment without mercy</u> that hath shown no mercy..."

KATIE WANTS TO TROT

Zeke told his boys the number of rows he wanted plowed before dinnertime, and they knew he intended them to finish on time.

They also knew that Katie, the mule, was stubborn. She would often refuse to obey the common commands taught mules. Commands like "gee" meaning to turn right, "haw" to turn left, and "whoa" to halt. Katie would come to the end of a row and sit refusing to get up and go. No amount of jabbing, pulling, or threatening would persuade her to cooperate.

Toward the end of the day, Katie did her squat at the end of a row, and the boys did what they could to get her up and going. Finally, Alton said, "I'm going to get a board from out behind the barn."

He returned with just the right size board to whack her between the eyes. He gave her one good lick, and she let out a yell they never forgot. From all of Katie's bellowing, Alton was sure he had killed his daddy's mule. As it turned out, that one whack was what was needed to get her up and going and with a new and improved attitude.

A few days later, Zeke said, "Boys, I don't know what's gotten into Katie. She's gotten to where, when she gets to the end of a row, she wants to trot!"

> ❖ **Proverbs 6:23** plainly tells us, "… reproofs of instruction are the way of life."

❖ **Proverbs 1:23** Turn you at my reproof: behold I will pour out my Spirit unto you, I will make my words known unto you.

Imagine having His Spirit poured out (not dribbled) unto you while you learn His word and all because you heeded His reproof!

❖ In contrast, **Proverbs 29:1** says, He that being often reproved hardeneth his neck, shall suddenly be destroyed, and that without remedy.

Having made many blunders on life's road, I remind the Lord frequently that, "Katie has gotten to where she wants to trot!"

KNOWING SCRIPTURE IS NOT ENOUGH

A prisoner in an Arkansas state penitentiary can all but yodel the Bible backwards. He is known for quoting large portions of scripture. He believes he is a member of the only church containing the limited number of 144,000 souls that will be saved and that there is no life after death except for these 144,000.

This is but one of his many erroneous beliefs. He has been deceived by a religious system that appeals to pride. This fault-ridden belief system convinced him that salvation is an "us four and no more" offer from God.

When speaking to the religious-without-relationship Jews, Jesus said, **(John 5:39,40-42)** "Search the scriptures; for in them ye think ye have eternal life; and they are they which testify of me. And ye will not come to me, that ye might have life. But I know you, that ye have not the love of God in you."

What can we conclude by this profound and yet brief discourse? These religious people had the word of God, they studied the word of God, they searched for eternal life through this word, and they did not love God. What a pathetic existence, and what a dreadful future!

God encourages us with these words which Paul wrote in **2nd Timothy 2:19**, "Nevertheless, the foundation of God standeth sure, having this seal, The Lord knoweth them that are His..."

And in **1st Corinthians 8:3** He added, "But if any man love God, the same is known of him."

2nd Thessalonians 2: tells of those who will be deceived in the end-time. Verse: 10, "And with all deceivableness of unrighteousness in them that perish, <u>because</u> they received not the love of the truth that they might be saved." Notice that they are deceived not because they did not have the truth but that they did not receive the love the truth. To put it bluntly, knowing scripture is not enough.

Like the Arkansas inmate who can quote lengthy scripture passages and yet will not come to Jesus that he might have eternal life. Jesus said in **Matthew 6:23** "...If, therefore, the light that is in thee be darkness, how great is that darkness!"

And **Luke 11:35** warns further, "Take heed, therefore, that the light which is in thee be not darkness."

And lastly, ponder these words written by the Apostle Paul and recorded in:
Romans 1:18 For the wrath of God is revealed from heaven against all ungodliness and unrighteousness of men, who hold the truth in unrighteousness.

Some search the scriptures to find promises to "claim." Remember, that the precious promises were given that we might be partakers of His divine nature and not so we could lay "claim" to any temporal earthly possession.

Embrace the love of the truth while you have opportunity. And remember that God knoweth them that are His.

LORD, I WILL FOLLOW WHEREVER YOU TELL ME TO GO
(Seigneur, Je Suivrai Ou Vous Me Dire D'aller)

Knowing her heart, He took her at her word as she vowed, "Lord I will follow wherever you tell me to go." She could not have dreamed of the number of souls that would be saved by her sincere promise.

In about 1950, after having a night vision of an angel, Jeanne Dufrene Magee awoke to find an angel standing at the foot of her bed. The angel gently touched her toes to fully awaken her. He said that Jesus wanted her to go to Dulac and preach the gospel.

These words spoken by the angel helped free Sister Magee from thinking that a re-married divorced woman was unworthy to proclaim His word. But the angel's direction didn't include specifics. Specifics like, where in the world was Dulac located? "Is that in Louisiana?" she asked.

When no further guidance came, she merely left her home in Covington, Louisiana and began driving south feeling the presence of the Lord. After driving seventy-one miles, she arrived in the town of Houma located in Terrebonne Parish in the southernmost part of the state. With confidence in God's guidance, she continued driving south until reaching the road's end at the community of Dulac thirteen miles south of Houma.

Only the area wasn't exactly a community then as it is today consisting of nearly 2,500 residents (51 percent Native-Americans and 49 percent Cajun-French) whose base of commerce is still fishing, trapping, and farming.

Then undeterred by the road ending, she got out of her car and walked through underbrush until she reached a bayou. There she saw a woman standing on the other side with her sons. The woman called out, "Are you the person God has sent?" She answered a heartfelt, "Yes, I am." Sister Magee knew full-well that she had been sent. So, without hesitating, she got into the skiff the woman had sent across the bayou with her young son, Leroy. The woman invited her home to visit. While enjoying coffee together, Sister Libby Parfait, as she was later known, told Sister Magee that she had been praying for someone to come and preach the word of God to the people there. Sister Magee shared her vision and of how she had been sent there to preach. The two women were amazed by how God had answered both their prayers, but they weren't nearly as amazed as they would be in the years to come. Their hearts were fused in a lifelong God-ordained friendship.

Sister Magee returned to Covington and told her husband she had found Dulac. Brother Magee knew of the angel's special message, and he was ready to support her wholeheartedly. As it happened, he already was working in the oil fields in south Louisiana, which was to make their transition easier.

Sister Magee spoke fluent French and was overjoyed to discover the local Houma Indians and Cajuns were both French-speaking people. This was but one of the "pre-equipping" provided by the Lord to make her way successful.

Sister Libby's home became a home-church during the next two years as Sister Magee faithfully proclaimed the uncompromised truth of God's word. Though having not preached before, she remained steadfast in God as she faced the prevailing powers of darkness that had bound many area people in Voodoo and demonic superstitions.

Sister Libby's house was filled with frequent prayer meetings. The spiritual atmosphere in Dulac improved as their prayers pierced, penetrated, and dispelled the thick layers of darkness that had long enshrouded the region.

Sister Libby gave the land where dedicated members built a church to worship in. That alone was a major accomplishment. It was in the new church that Sister Magee was to confront a God-hating spirit from the world of darkness.

While preparing to preach, she saw a witch doctor coming toward her in the center aisle with a gun stuck in his pants. This witch doctor had decided that the community of Dulac wasn't big enough for both Sister Magee and him. The only feasible solution was to remove this preacher-woman whose ministry had threatened his livelihood. He was to discover that Sister Magee was also armed but with a much superior weapon –

The NAME OF JESUS!

She began to preach engulfed with a heavy anointing as her husband and other men kept a close eye on the would-be assassin. Under the control of Satan, the witch doctor refused to sit down as he heckled a preacher-woman who refused to be heckled. She instructed the devil-bound man to, "Either shoot me or sit down and listen to what the Lord has to say." Much to the relief of the church-members, he slithered onto a pew and remained quiet.

Before the service concluded, this man was set free by the power of Jesus name and the preaching of His word. He fell to his knees begging forgiveness and asking to be saved. He was marvelously saved and delivered that very night!

The church grew to a sizable congregation. God put it in Sister Magee's heart to hold prayer meetings in her home. Later, He instructed her to conduct prayer meetings in other homes as well. Many were saved, delivered, and healed during the duration of these prayer meetings.

Sister Magee and her husband, Brother Merton "Red" Magee were to remain there for twenty-two years as faithful and well-beloved ministers of the gospel. Brother Magee stayed by her side assisting her in obeying God's call. He also played the guitar as she played the piano.
Her adult-son, L. T. Candies, visited after they moved to Dulac. He left crying after seeing their improvised living conditions. Their loved-filled home was actually a shack without even an air-conditioner to combat the brutal climate. L. T. knew the home they had left before going where God had sent them had been well-built and air-conditioned.

After the church was built, Sister and Brother Magee lived in two of its rooms, one on either side of the altar.

Later, they built a nice air-conditioned parsonage on land behind the church.

Their ministry did not end at Dulac. After leaving there, they pastored a church in Houma before taking a church in Covington. What a blessing this couple was to the Lord and to His people.

Their testimony shows that the Lord has plans for His people even when they feel unworthy; for He knows what is in their hearts, and He knows what He desires to enable them to do.

> **There once was a woman sent from God, whose name was**
> **JEANNE DUFRENE CANDIES MAGEE.**
>
> **She loved God and she loved people.**
> **B: June 23, 1905**
> **D: March 7, 1992**

Update:

God's work continues in the community of Dulac. Sister Libby and her children, including Leroy, who brought the skiff to get Sister Magee, have remained faithful to God and the work of the church. Her entire family also remains lovingly close to the family of Sister Magee.

Brother Tim Nuckles had just arrived in Louisiana following the August 29, 2005 Hurricane Katrina catastrophe to assume the position of Administrative Bishop of the Louisiana Church of God when God spoke a word to him while in prayer. The word spoken repeatedly to his spirit was, "Dulac." He wondered if there was a place named Dulac. He stopped praying to ask an assistant if there was a Dulac in Louisiana. When the assistant located Dulac on a state map, Brother Nuckles knew that God had something extraordinary for the whole area. Brother Nuckles coordinated the rebuilding of the heavily damaged Dulac church in the aftermath of the storm utilizing volunteers from Virginia, Tennessee, and other states in a selfless effort for the glory of God.

Our God has a special interest in the work He has begun, protected, and loved all these many years.

To God be the glory!

LORD, PITY US

A bristled shock wave traveled through everyone in the prayer circle, everyone, that is, but me. They were all deeply offended by my prayer, whereas I was saddened by their staunch rejection of acknowledging who we truly are as recipients of God's unmerited favor and mercy.

With a contrite heart, I had begun by praying, "Father, pity us." Their mortified reaction drowned the remainder of my prayer. After all, these were people of great faith and power who did not need God's pity.

My God-inspired prayer had come from King David's plea written nearly three thousand years ago and recorded in **Psalm 103**. The twenty-two verses in this psalm contain the phrase "them that fear Him" three times. The entire Bible records this phrase only thirteen times, and, of the thirteen, twelve are in psalms written by King David.

Verses :11 and :12 are as follows: For as the heavens are high above the earth, so great is His mercy toward them that fear Him. As far as the east is from the west, so far hath He removed our transgressions from us.

Our Creator knows the distance between north and south is measurable and that the distance between east and west cannot be measured. King David's choice of words were not accidental.

I hope you need the God who can remove your transgressions as far as the east is from the west to pity you. The Hebrew word (#7355) "pitieth," means "to love in an especially compassionate way." God loves His children who fear Him in this way, and He wants them, in turn, to love Him as they should.

:13-14 As a father <u>pitieth</u> his children, so the Lord <u>pitieth</u> them that fear him. For he knoweth our frame; he remembereth that we are dust.

Being "clothed in humility" is light years away from being "puffed up" with vanity and pride.

Consider the admonition found in:
1st Peter 5:5-6 ... be clothed in humility; for God resisteth the proud, and giveth grace to the humble. Humble yourselves, therefore, under the mighty hand of God, that he may exalt you in due time.

Unsurpassed sweet communion with the Father is enjoyed by those who walk close by His side. Having found this to be true, I determined years ago that I would choose to lag behind those who bristle at the thought of having God pity them.

Let's remember the cry of Kind David's heart found in:
Psalm 39:5 Thou hast made my days as a hand-breadth, and mine age is as nothing before thee; verily every man in his best state is altogether vanity.

LORD, TEACH US TO SAVOR THE THINGS THAT ARE OF YOU!

Matthew 16:21-23 From that time forth began Jesus to show unto his disciples, how he must go unto Jerusalem, and suffer many things from the elders and chief priests and scribes, and be killed, and be raised again the third day. Then Peter took him, and began to rebuke him, saying, Be it far from thee, Lord; this shall not be unto thee. <u>But</u> he turned and said unto Peter; Get thee behind me, Satan. Thou art an offense unto me; for thou savourest not the things that are of God, but those that are of men.

Though hard to envision, Peter actually spoke these words of rebuke to Jesus who in turn delivered His strongest recorded reprimand. To put it in modern terms, they just weren't on the same page.

Notice the tremendous change in Peter after having received the power of the Holy Ghost. When speaking before an amazed and doubting crowd recorded in **Acts 2:23**, he states, "Him, being delivered by the <u>determinate counsel and foreknowledge of God</u>, ye have taken, and by wicked hands have crucified and slain..." By these words, Peter is clearly declaring that he had begun to "savor" the things that be of God.

Included in the words spoken by Jesus to Peter following His resurrection are these:
John 21:18 ... thou shalt stretch forth thy hands, and another shall gird thee, and carry thee where thou wouldest not.

John is careful to give us understanding of this scripture by stating in verse:19, "This spoke he signifying by what death he should glorify God."

Could it be that God wants us to understand that He can receive glory by our death? The determinate counsel and foreknowledge of God would later deliver Peter unto a martyr's death. What an overwhelming thought!

- ❖ **Psalm 116:15** Precious in the sight of the Lord is the death of His saints.

  Lord, teach us to savor the things that are of You!

LORD, WAS IT ME?

"Lord, was it me?" was the anguished cry from the grandmother's heart. The funeral of her oldest daughter's firstborn six-month old infant had been a few days earlier. Numbed by the months of care giving while grieving, Sharon was too depleted to actually pray as she wanted. Exhausted and drained with no more tears to shed, she sat at her kitchen table in a rare moment of solitude and wondered.

With four other daughters still living at home, Sharon and her husband found little quiet time. And, for the last six months, since the birth of little Christian Grey, their normal routine had become a thing of the past. Their new routine was to join with other family members committed to ensuring little Christian would always be held and rocked in the neonatal intensive care unit. This loving vow might seem hard to be accomplished. It wasn't though, as each considered their time with her to be a privilege.

Christian was born with "malabsorption syndrome" which meant her body was unable to absorb the nutrients needed to sustain life. Everyone knew she would never leave the hospital. They would have to wait until God called for her.

Sharon drove her daughter to the hospital for what was to be their last earthly moments with Christian. She watched through the neonatal intensive care unit's window as her daughter tenderly held her firstborn. Sharon watched as she put her hand over Christian's eyes and lovingly closed her eyelids. She then called for the nurse before placing Christian in her crib. God had called and released her from the confines of flesh.

In the weeks that followed, Sharon needed to ask the Lord questions had been left unasked while the care routine was taking its toll. Now in the private crucible of soul-searching she asked, "Lord, was it me? Have I done anything to cause this? I have failed You many times. Was her death because of something I have done?" The Lord tenderly spoke, "You are too young to understand." His peace then settled her heart.

Just as Jesus told His disciples in:
John 16:12 I have many things to say unto you, but ye cannot bear them now.

Yes, we are too young to understand all that God determines best. But we are never too young to trust Him and believe that He works all things together for the good to them that love God, to them that are the called according to His purpose. **(Romans 8:28)**

Paul declared in **Romans 11:33**, "Oh, the depth of the riches both of the wisdom and knowledge of God! How unsearchable are His judgments, and His ways are past finding out!"

A few years later, Sharon's second oldest daughter, Lydia, was praying in the church's prayer room when she looked up and saw a vision of Christian standing in the glory world wearing a long glowing white gown. Only she wasn't a six-month old infant. She was a full-grown young woman.

Lydia struggled to transmit love to Christian, but all of her projected emotion merely bounced back. Christian was so full she just couldn't hold anymore. Lydia asked, "Oh, Christian am I going to be able to marry and have children before the coming of the Lord?" Christian laughed and said, "Oh, no, no. Don't even think about your own life. Just love God. I have to go now. He's calling me."

"<u>Just love God</u>" could be some of the best advice given to anyone at any time. Lydia did go on in her own life, and she just loved God. And, yes, Lydia did marry a godly young man. Their firstborn, a son, was born in 1985.

MERCY STOOD STILL AND COMMANDED

The Aramaic prefix, "<u>Bar</u>" means "son of." Jesus referred to Peter as "Simon <u>Bar</u>-jona" (Greek #3920) meaning he was the son of Jonah. Likewise, the disciple called <u>Bar</u>tholomew (Greek #918) was the son of Tolmai.

The four gospels speak of Jesus healing unnamed blind people. However, only the Gospel of Mark **(10:46)** identifies one as being "blind <u>Bar</u>timaeus (Greek #924), the son of Timæus, who sat by the wayside begging."

As Jesus came out of Jericho with His disciples and a great number of people, while on His way to His last appearance in Jerusalem before the Passover, He graciously healed this beggar man.

The gospels are rippled with descriptions of ordinary people, like Bartimaeus, living mundane lives of hopelessness. Ordinary people, that is, until Jesus does something <u>extra-ordinary</u> in their lives. Mundane, that is, until Jesus passes by. Hopeless until He heeds their cry for mercy.

Without a doubt, Bartimaeus had heard and believed reports concerning Jesus and had hoped that he would somehow be helped by Him. When he was told that Jesus was passing by, he began to cry out, "Jesus, thou son of David; have mercy on me," as many rebuked him and charged him to hold his peace."

Knowing Jesus was his only hope, he cried (Greek #2896 meaning 'to scream') the more - a great deal more. Since this was a big deal in his life, he cried a great deal more. Wouldn't we all?

The scriptures beginning in **Mark 10:46** tell us that Jesus was accompanied by His disciples and a great number of people. Is it any wonder that this lowly beggar had to scream to be heard?

Jesus, hearing his cry for <u>mercy; stood still, and commanded</u> Bartimaeus to be called to him. **(Mark 10:49)** This is the only recorded instance where Jesus commanded someone be brought to Him.

When you need His full attention, recognize Him as your only hope, and cry out to Him for mercy. When your entire being is focused on Him, His entire focus will be on you.

After Jesus commanded he be brought to Him, the same people who had, at the first, charged him to hold his peace, then said, "Be of good comfort; rise, He calleth thee." What glorious words!

Bartimaeus had never known any comfort. Now he is told to rise from the trash heap of his existence and come to Jesus and all because he cried for mercy in faith believing that Jesus would heal him. Showing his eagerness, he arose casting away the garment that identified him as a beggar.

My friend, we must do the same. Throw off the old identity and put on the new; be willing and eager to get up and to go on with Jesus leaving the old identity behind.

2nd Corinthians 5:17 states, "Therefore, if any man be in Christ, he is a new creature; old things are passed away; behold, all things are become new."

Jesus then acknowledged that he was healed because of his faith. Faith produces both rest and action. Notice that Bartimaeus immediately received his sight, and that he followed Jesus on the way.

Jesus was headed to His divine appointment in Jerusalem. We can only wonder if the grateful Bartimaeus followed Him all the way up Calvary's hill. We wonder, too, if he saw the empty tomb on Resurrection Morning.

MY SON, GOD WILL PROVIDE HIMSELF A LAMB

Hebrews 9:22 states, "... without the shedding of blood is no remission (of sin). **Leviticus 17:11** states, "For the life of the flesh is in the blood... for it is the blood that maketh an atonement for the soul."

Genesis 22 tells of God instructing Abraham, contrary to Levitical Law, to take his only son Isaac to the land of Moriah and offer him as a burnt offering. What a test for them both! This is an actually event which occurred in approximately 1784 B.C.

After traveling for three days, Abraham lifted up his eyes and saw the place afar off. Abraham and Isaac went together as Isaac carried the wood for the offering and Abraham carried the fire and a knife. Soon Isaac asked his father, "Behold the fire and the wood: but where is the lamb for a burnt offering?" No truer words than the answer given by Abraham could have been spoken. He said, "My son, God will provide himself a lamb for a burnt offering." He certainly did, didn't He?

In **Genesis 4:4**, a lamb was offered for the sin of one man (Abel.) **Exodus 12:3** states that the blood of a spotless lamb was offered for the sin of each household. In **Leviticus 16:29-34**, a lamb was offered for the sin of the nation. Lastly, **John 1:29** records John saying, "Behold the Lamb of God that taketh away the sin of the world."

Have you seen a picture of a shepherd carrying a lamb across his shoulders without realizing why the shepherd is carrying the lamb? This lamb may have been a rebellious lamb who had strayed from the fold many times not responding to the shepherd's voice. By his willful wandering, he may become trapped in a crevasse or ravine. The shepherd hastens to his distressed cry knowing that his cry may also bring a predator. To chasten a repeatedly rebellious lamb, the shepherd will break its leg. The shepherd will then carry the lamb across his shoulders until he is completely healed. Isn't that just like Jesus, to carry us until we are completely healed?

During this time of healing, the lamb learns to eat out of the shepherd's hand; he learns the shepherd's smell, his touch, and his voice. When the lamb is fully restored, he will be willing to stay close by the shepherd's side. If the chastened lamb continued in willful rebellion and, especially if other lambs begin to follow, the shepherd will slaughter it.

King David had been a shepherd boy, and he understood the chastening of the Lord when he wrote his great psalm of repentance. In **Psalm 51:8**, he pleaded "...that the bones that thou hast broken may rejoice." The shepherd king of Israel understood how God had dealt with him.

Exodus 12:46 and **Numbers 9:12** instruct Jews not to break a bone of a sacrificial lamb used in a Passover Celebration. Could this by why Jesus, the Lamb of God, did not have His legs broken? The men crucified with Jesus were malefactors and, as such, had their legs broken.

John 19:36 in quoting **Psalm 34:20** says, "For these things were done, that the scripture should be fulfilled, A bone of him shall not be broken."

To be an acceptable sacrifice, a lamb had to be publicly examined for three days prior to the Passover Celebration to prove it was without spot or blemish and had no broken bones. Could this be why Jesus showed Himself openly in Jerusalem for three days prior to fulfilling the will of God?

Blessed be JESUS, the Lamb of God.

PRAY, AND GO ON

Of all the advice I've received, "Pray, and go on," has got to be some of the best. Years ago I was attending a church that was under constant assault from Satan and from unruly members dominated by the evil-one. Those who were praying engaged in continuous warfare that went from one fatiguing tumult to another.

It was easy to become distraught, perplexed, and discouraged. But each time I would say something like, "Oh, what are we going to do?" to an older woman, she would always say, "I don't know. Let's just pray and go on." After a few tumults, I began to realize that this was her standard advice and that it was good advice.

Whatever the problem, whatever the dilemma, whatever the seemingly impossibility we are faced with, the answer is always the same; pray, and go on. He is God. He knows more about it than you do. He can do more in a moment that you can in a lifetime.

"Pray, and go on," is not, "Pray, and give up," or, "Pray, and stew in it." It is simply saying - pray releasing your concern. Let Him resolve it His way and in His time. Whatever concerns you, concerns Him, and He has promised to perfect that which concerns you. After all, you are His workmanship.

Isaiah 26:3 Thou wilt keep him in perfect peace, whose mind is stayed upon thee, because he trusteth in thee.

Philippians 4:6-7 Be anxious for nothing, but in everything, by prayer and supplication with thanksgiving, let your request be known unto God. And the peace of God, which passeth all understanding, shall keep your hearts and minds through Christ Jesus.

The word "keep" in this scripture is a Greek (#5432) word, which means "to post a guard or a sentinel."

How awesome is our God to assure us that through prayer our hearts and minds will be kept, guarded and watched over as a sentinel would do.

SHE HATH DONE WHAT SHE COULD

All four gospels tell of the alabaster box of ointment and the sinner woman who used the ointment to anoint Jesus prior to His death. Only the Gospel of John identifies her as Mary, the sister of Martha and Lazarus.

Studying the four gospel accounts of this event is very intriguing. The actions and reactions of those involved yields lessons of significance. One is that of Mary of Bethany, who did not have the benefit of private instruction, consultation, or exposition by Jesus, and yet was the <u>only person</u> to comprehend His having clearly stated that He would be scourged and crucified. She alone was able to grasp His foretelling because she had sat at His feet and listened.

- ❖ **Luke 7:38** says that she stood weeping <u>behind</u> Him, obviously not seeing herself as worthy to appear before Him.
- ❖ **Mark 14:5** reveals that they (the disciples too) murmured against her.
- ❖ **Matthew 26:8** says that the disciples reacted with indignation (Greek word #23, meaning "sore, displeased") against her.

Mary felt convicted of her sins and recognized her need for cleansing. Jesus understood that she was among people who murmured against. He defended her actions by saying, "Let her alone," and "She hath done what she could." **(Mark 14:6,8)**

The other women, including Mary Magdalene, Salome, and the other Mary, all came to His sepulcher after His burial arriving while it was still dark. And, yet, they arrived too late to anoint Him, because He had already been anointed by Mary who "hath done what she could."

The blind, well-beloved writer of over 8,000 hymns, Fannie Crosby, died February 12, 1915 at ninety-five years of age. These words are engraved on her tombstone in Bridgeport, Connecticut, "She hath done what she could."

What a commendable statement to be made about anyone. Particularly of someone, like you, who has faced many perplexing difficulties. And, like Mary of Bethany, whose actions showed she comprehended what Jesus was saying when others did not, you, too, have the privilege of sitting at His dear feet.

When I began walking the pilgrim pathway, I was void of spiritual understanding. I attempted to fill this void with church seminar after seminar, with volumes of error-laced teachings, and with much praying amiss.

Finally, after reading **Proverbs 13:15**, which says, "Good understanding giveth favor, but the way of transgressors is hard," I asked, "Lord, Your word says that the way of transgressors is hard. I have come a hard way. My walk in you has not been easy. Are you saying that I am in transgression?" His instantaneous reply broke my heart but provided the needed course correction. He said, "I would have taught you all you needed to know had you sat at my feet, but you …" His speech trailed off in a fill-in-the-blank mode. Our non-condemning God left it to me to insert the words I then knew to be true. I shudder when thinking of the years wasted running here and there doing "Christian things" that I thought were bringing me closer to God but were not. I had over-looked the supreme comfort zone of sitting at His feet and being taught all I needed to know.

Having it said by the Lord, "She hath done what she could" will be reward enough for those who have done what they could.

SHE IS NOT PUSHING THIS

Even though our eyes met for only a millisecond, Brother Ramsey and I both knew what was happening. I was struggling to comprehend what the Lord had interrupted my "current reality" to reveal.

I hung my head down with my eyes closed to help block out the church service. Like a message rolling on an old ticker tape, the Lord shared His grief.

I glanced back over my shoulder to Brother and Sister Ramsey sitting behind me. They knew God was speaking to me, and, without words, they understood that I was momentarily overwhelmed and could not speak.

Then I shared His message directed to Brother Ramsey. The Lord had said, "You have thought she was pushing this, and you have wondered why. She is not pushing this. I am doing this. You cannot calculate the amount of evil done against her." He also let me know that He wanted this evil judged in man's court of law.

Older male half-siblings had horribly sexually abused her throughout her childhood. She could not bear children due to scar tissue that even surgery could not mend. But the scars left on her heart were even worse. However, the Great Physician has worked wonderfully to heal in only ways that He could.

The state's Child Protection Services failed to provide her protection when notified repeatedly of the situation at home. The adults in her life were not what they should have been either. When her pleas for help were ignored, she learned to endure. Well into her adulthood, she began to sense this whole matter needed to be acknowledged.

Now, years later and after filing a lawsuit against the state's agency, her husband was wondering, "Why is she pushing this?" It is awesome how the Lord Himself stepped in to correct his thinking.

I wouldn't want to speculate on why He chose to direct Sister Ramsey's steps the way He did. I do know that she had been greatly strengthened during the five years prior by the love of a godly husband. Perhaps God was waiting until she was strong enough to slay this giant.

Sister Ramsey won the suit and a small monetary judgment. She felt vindicated at last. This was a major step in the healing God had begun. But this is not the end of His judgment. There will be more to come for all involved in this evil matter both in this life or the next.

God had said that we would not be able to calculate the evil done against her, and we know His calculator far exceeds anything we can imagine. His judgments are just, and He is greatly to be feared.

SHE STORMED THE THRONE ROOM

The picture of an exceptionally attractive young woman caught my eye as I glanced at the "Religion" section of our newspaper. The caption announced she would be speaking to an area congregation concerning her personal triumph of faith. It was interesting enough for me to want to know more so I began reading the entire article.

Belinda Stone, the article read, had prevailed over doubt and fear while struggling to find her true identity in Christ. She had been raised in what she called "a small town religious atmosphere" and attended the same denomination as most of its residents. Looking back on her early church experience, she joked that it was only "Sunday day-care."

She and her high school sweetheart had married young and within five years were the parents of two daughters. Everyone in their "Mayberry lifestyle" community thought all was well in her home and life. Belinda, however, found that she was not comfortable being married to a man. Abandoning her husband and daughters, she struck out to "find herself" within her new lesbian lifestyle.

The interviewer wrote of the deep anguish she felt as she struggled to reconcile her lifestyle to Biblical teaching. The satisfaction and pride she experienced by openly becoming "who she truly was" quieted the raging inner conflict of her soul.

Belinda knew enough scripture to know that believers can go directly before the throne of grace. Desperately wanting to shed her guilt and shame, she jumped to her feet when an assertive plan of action formed in her mind. She thought that by taking this one step she would forever end the relentless guilt and shame that had plagued her conscience.

With an incredible burst of empowerment, she made the decision to "STORM THE THRONE ROOM" and confidently tell the Lord, "God, I come boldly before your throne and declare to you that THIS is who I am and THIS is who I love!" In that moment she said that she felt released from torment and free to be "who she really was."

In the years that followed, this deceived woman became quite an in demand articulate speaker at "churches" that are fueled by such error. Yet, there was nothing in her "testimony" that could "pass the smell test" much less a scripture test. Had Belinda prayed verbatim the scripture she misquoted, she may not have been so confident.

Hebrews 4:15-16 For we have not an high priest who cannot be touched with the feeling of our infirmities, but was in all points tempted like as we are, yet without sin. Let us, therefore, come boldly unto the throne of grace, that we may obtain mercy, and find grace to help in time of need.

Belinda's high level of impenitence had torpedoed all hope of obtaining the mercy and grace she needed.

Mercy and grace for believers are obtained by humility and not by storming the throne room. For those who are walking in the fear of the Lord, hearing someone say they "stormed the throne room" is more than a little unsettling.

Remember, too, that when the Apostle John saw the Lord he "fell at his feet as dead." **(Revelation 1:17)**

Old Testament, as well as New Testament, scriptures denounce homosexuality as an absolute abomination which God in no way will tolerate. He will, however, deliver, cleanse, and save any repentant believer who earnestly seeks to be delivered, cleansed, and saved.

Sorely lacking in humility and not recognizing her need for mercy and grace had brought Belinda to a depraved condition. Trusting in her own self-righteousness, she failed to submit to God and receive the imputed righteousness of Christ.

- **2nd Timothy 3:13** But evil men and seducers shall become worse and worse, deceiving, and being deceived.
- **Romans 10:3** For they, being ignorant of God's righteousness, and going about to establish their own righteousness, have not submitted themselves unto the righteousness of God.
- **Leviticus 18:22** Thou shalt not lie with mankind, as with womankind: it is an abomination.
- **Leviticus 20:13** If a man also lie with mankind, as he lieth with a woman, both of them have committed an abomination: they shall surely be put to death; their blood shall be upon them.
- **Romans 1:26** For this cause God gave them up unto vile affections; for even their women did change the natural use for that which is against nature.

Let's consider Belinda's assessment of her hometown church as being no more than a "Sunday day-care." The failure of this church to teach the love of the truth and to lead its members into a holy relationship with God is reprehensible. However; it could have been that Belinda just didn't "get the message."

Tragically, someone who has the holy word of God and who does not embrace the love of the truth is throwing open the door of their heart to deception and debauchery.

Proverbs 16:6 By mercy and truth iniquity is purged; and by the fear of the Lord men depart from evil.

A wholesome, continual cleansing is experienced by those who walk in the fear of the Lord.

1st John 1:6-7 If we say that we have fellowship with Him, and <u>walk</u> in darkness, we lie, and do not the truth; but if we <u>walk</u> in the light, as He is in the light, we have fellowship one with another, and the blood of Jesus Christ, His Son, <u>cleanseth</u> us from all sin.

Notice the active repetitive verbs, "<u>walk</u>," and "<u>cleanseth</u>." They actually mean "walking" and "cleansing" to be continuous actions.

Oh, dear pilgrim, do not neglect such a great salvation! It is a complete salvation from sin as believers continue to be cleansed as they walk in Him.

The Bible does not contain any scripture inviting saints or sinners to "storm the throne room." However, it does contain many invitations from the heart of God.

A heart-rending example is found in **Isaiah 1:18** where God pleads, "Come now, and let us reason together, saith the Lord: though your sins be as scarlet, they shall be as white as snow; though they be red like crimson, they shall be as wool."

SHE'S DISQUALIFIED

If she had heard these words spoken about herself, she may not have believed them even though they were spoken by the Holy Ghost. She also may not have believed the words that trailed afterward either.

We were standing near each other in the church's Fellowship Hall. I was thinking of how the church needed someone to act as a wedding coordinator. The church had had an unusual number of weddings lately making the need for a coordinator quite evident.

As I glanced at Ellen, I thought, "Oh, she's a good organizer. Besides that she would be able to handle any would-be "bride-zillars." I'll just ask her to do it." Even though I knew she had a problem with an over-active tongue and would sometimes maneuver to increase her status within the church, I was unwisely willing to ask her to consider taking on this responsibility. (Shame on me!)

The Holy Ghost abruptly prevented me from approaching her by interjecting, "She is disqualified." And, as my mind tried to wrap around that statement, He added, "from further service."

Since then I have thought many times about how serious and irrevocable His judgments are and about how unaware we are that we are being observed and judged. Yes, there is plenteous mercy and abundant grace. There is also the severity of God.

Someone masquerading in a servant-charade is not hidden from God. He does not need a lightbulb to see through the darkness lurking in the recesses of our hearts. But He does need our permission to enter those recesses to do the work of cleansing.

King David acknowledged his need for cleansing when he wrote in **Psalm 19:12**, "...Cleanse thou me from secret faults."

Our faults may remain secret and not confessed until God illuminates them. We should welcome the chance to have our inner heart, motives, and desires made known and made right by our Creator God.

Much of life's experience can be summarized as an "elimination round." Many enter the race attempting to obtain immortality but miss their goal by being self-serving rather than learning to be a true Christ-like servant.

John 2:23-25 ... many believed in his name, when they saw the miracles which he did. But Jesus did not commit himself unto them, because he knew all men, and needed not that any should testify of man; for he knew what was in man.

While in imprisoned in Rome, the Apostle Paul wrote to the church at Philippi saying he would send Timothy who was proven to be a servant. But, when referring to certain others, Paul wrote in **Philippians 2:21**, "For all seek their own, and not the things which are Jesus Christ's."

And, speaking of seeking, consider the words of Paul: **Colossians 3:1** If ye, then, be risen with Christ, <u>seek</u> those things which are above where Christ sitteth on the right hand of God.

The Christian should not be involved in seeking vain-glory. Rather than be preoccupied with these carnal pursuits, let us focus on our acceptability to Him. After all, when your last breath leaves your body, nothing else will matter forever.

SHE'S RESTING, COULD YOU CALL BACK LATER?

Making preparations for our family reunion necessitated my calling an elderly cousin, Ruth Perkins. When I called around 10 a.m., her husband, John, answered the phone and in a hushed tone whispered, "She's resting. Could you call back later?" "Oh, of course. I am so sorry to have troubled you," was my response. I dismissed the thought that her resting at that hour was unusual.

Sometime after two in the afternoon, I called again only to be told the same thing. This was a little odd. The following day I decided to call another cousin to see if there was anything wrong. I closed my eyes, shook my head, and felt such deep compassion when told that Ruth had not been "resting." She had been in a diabetic coma and that she had died during the night.

We briefly discussed how this couple had drifted from the love of the truth and out into error. It's interesting that I used the word "error," because their religious system teaches that all sickness is error and doesn't actually exist. Medical help of any kind is greatly discouraged. The same is true of death. Death is denied; therefore it doesn't exist either.

Ruth's heartbroken husband, still holding to his faulty beliefs, was to follow her in death a few months later.

Family members had long before given up hope of reaching either Ruth or John. They were as unwavering in their religious persuasion as any deceived person could be. It offered a comfortable belief system with the promise of divine health as long as you denied evidence of anything contrary. You are safe within this system as long as you maintain a high level of denial. It's a sure-to-fail tragic way of coping with unpleasant realities.

It may be that their staunch denial of illness and death had its roots in fear. **Hebrews 2:15** says that by destroying him who had the power of death, he (Jesus) delivered them who through fear of death, were all their lifetimes subject to bondage.

God intends for His people to conquer; not to cope through false beliefs. His word gives us sufficient counsel to do so.

- ❖ **2ⁿᵈ Corinthians 13:5**   Examine yourselves, whether you are in the faith; prove yourselves.

- ❖ **1ˢᵗ John 4:1**   Beloved, believe not every spirit, but test (try) the spirits whether they are of God…

And the Apostle John uses these words when writing to his friend, Gaius, recorded for us in **3ʳᵈ John :4**, "I have no greater joy than to hear that my children walk in truth."

Walking in His marvelous truth leaves no room for deception. Make it your goal to guard your heart with all diligence continually.

SO RUN THAT YE MAY OBTAIN

According to an article published by the Museum of Hoaxes, after having obtained the third fastest time ever recorded for a female runner, Rosie Ruiz was remarkably sweat-free as she climbed the winner's podium to accept her wreath at the April 21, 1980 Boston Marathon.

Race officials doubted her victory immediately since no one could remember seeing her in the race, race checkpoint monitors hadn't seen her, nor had any other runners. Numerous photographs taken during the race failed to contain any sign of Rosie. Her absence was overwhelming.

Finally, witnesses from the crowd came forward to reveal that they had seen her jump into the race during its final half-mile. Rosie was then disqualified and stripped of her victory, and the title awarded to the real winner.

- ❖ **1st Corinthians 9:24** Know ye not that they who run in a race run all, but one receiveth the prize? So run, that ye may obtain.
- ❖ **2nd Timothy 2:5** And if a man strive for masteries (as an athlete,) yet he is not crowned, except he strive lawfully.
- ❖ **Hebrews 12:1** Wherefore, seeing we also are compassed about with a great a cloud of witnesses, let us lay aside every weight, and the sin which doth easily beset us, and let us run with patience the race that is set before us.

You have entered this race to win. Like Rosie, there will be witnesses to testify of the quality of race you run.

Endeavor to persevere in serving Him wholeheartedly with godly sincerity.

Revelation 3:11 Behold, I come quickly; hold fast which thou hast, that no man take thy crown.

SOMEONE IMPORTANT HAS DIED

Not thinking of anything in particular, I drove past an inner city section headed toward Wal-Mart. I took a quick look to the left at a blighted area of town as I slowed for a traffic light. There were vehicles parked at a church and on either side of the road spilling out onto the highway.

An unexpected rush of joy flooded my soul, as I thought, "Oh, wonderful! Someone is getting married." A second thought quickly came, "Two p.m. on a Friday is an unusual time to be getting married." Then the Spirit of the Living God spoke and shared the joyous news, "Someone important has died."

A blessed event had occurred without the world noticing. I pondered over this announcement and wondered about the glorious homecoming this saint had received.

Knowing that to be absent from the body is to be present with the Lord, I thought of the words of an old hymn written by R. H. Cornelius, "Tears all past, home at last, ever to rejoice."

Perhaps this saint's life had been rather mundane and uneventful. Mundane and uneventful that is to those who do not comprehend a life hidden in the bosom of God.

The soul of this person had been a life He had called out of darkness and drawn into fellowship with Him. What a privileged life! This saint had surely walked hand in hand with God glorifying Him through much adversity.

This "someone" whom He said was "important," was not someone who was important to our city, state, nation, or world. There wasn't a police motorcade escort to the cemetery. The president did not order flags to be flown at half-staff. The world did not stand still and take notice of this saint's departure. <u>But God did</u>. He had prepared a mansion for this important someone long ago.

- ❖ **James 2: 5** Hath not God chosen the poor of this world to be rich in faith and heirs of the kingdom which He hath promised to them that love Him?

- ❖ **Psalm 116:15** Precious in the sight of the Lord is the death of His saints.

These words are written to honor God for sharing His joy with me that day, and to acknowledge the devotion of the saint who had departed.

And they are written to help you understand that you are someone important to God. You may never be honored, respected, appreciated, or even loved in this world. But, remember, this life is but a vapor and it will soon pass away.

God knows your heart, and He is waiting to honor your love and faithful service to Him and to others.

SORRY, MA'AM, YOU HAVE THE WRONG NUMBER

A phone call interrupted a monotonous day at the office. Realizing the caller hadn't intended to call a plumbing company, I said, "Sorry, ma'am, you have the wrong number." The pleasant-voiced caller apologized and said she had wanted to reach another company with a similar name. "No problem," I responded as I searched the phone book for the number she needed.

What happened next remains a mystery to us both today more than thirty years later. We began a conversation and soon discovered that we both loved Jesus. Even though our lives had been of entirely different experiences, we immediately found common ground on which to enjoy genuine fellowship; that is, we found that we were fellows-in-the-same-ship.

Before our initial conversation was concluded with prayer, I learned that Gwen Perry was a well-educated African-American. Over time, as our friendship grew, I was to learn that her love and devotion to the good of others was only surpassed by her love for God.

Neither of us can remember why I mentioned to her that I lived in Denham Springs located in the neighboring parish of Livingston. Gwen's voice lowered, as if amazed, as she recalled a recent experience she had while seeking help in Denham Springs for a young woman pregnant out of wedlock. She had cautiously approached a church sponsored outreach asking assistance for the woman and her unborn child. She was relieved to receive a wholehearted welcome from the outreach personnel who lovingly moved quickly to meet the woman's immediate and future needs. Gwen was painfully aware that this might not have been the case in the "old south."

Our sporadic telephone-friendship continued although sometimes it was just a greeting to say, "I've been thinking of you." We would share like schoolgirls the joyful things we had experienced in God as we each walked the pilgrim pathway. Though there may have been a lapse of even a few years, our friendship would be instantly renewed by the sound of each other's voice on the phone.

If Gwen could not reach out to everyone around her, she would be a miserable person. She must communicate God's love to others by whatever means available. Her love is expressed in newspaper writing, publishing, and distributing, as well as in book writing, Bible study groups, and prayer meetings.

From time to time, a copy of Gwen's self-published community newspaper would arrive in my mail. It would be filled with the reporting of all sorts of "people news." Her love for God and others could be felt in every article and seen in every picture. This was one of the ways God had ordained to bless others through her.

Thoughts of Gwen had danced across my mind for several days before I called her in February 2009. I had not sensed anything was wrong or that she was troubled in anyway. We each quickly shared our "catch up" data. She then told me of her husband's eighteen month struggle with cancer but quickly added that they were believing God for his healing. Even though Cleo seemed to be holding his own, his doctor had told them he had only a short time to live.

Not disregarding the doctor's assessment, Cleo and Gwen remained strong in their faith and trusted that the God of eternity was working on their behalf. Before hanging up the phone, I promised to keep in touch and to pray.
Much to my surprise, eight days later, I read Cleo's obituary notice in the newspaper, which included a picture of this handsome man whom I had never met. Because of a work obligation, I knew I wouldn't be able to attend his funeral service. I also knew I was not going to miss his wake service even though it would be in the northern part of an adjacent parish.

My husband mapped out the course and off I went. Just as I had expected, the large funeral home was packed with people wanting to honor Cleo and comfort Gwen and their family. The atmosphere was filled with jubilation. Yes, there was sorrow, but it did not outweigh the presence of God. Nothing can parallel the exuberant celebration of a saint's home going. The comfort and strength supplied by God's Spirit and through His people was amazing. I glanced at the people standing near Cleo's coffin and wondered which one was Gwen. Then the realization came; I would have to ask someone to tell me which person was Gwen, my special friend of over thirty years. It struck me as sort of funny, like an inside joke, that I had no way of recognizing my God-given telephone friend. A man who was standing in the receiving line ahead of me pointed Gwen out. She was just as I had imagined her.

The sound of my greeting brought immediate rejoicing to us both. We hugged, giggled, and stood back to look at each other; then we hugged and giggled some more. Surely many mourners were curious at the sight.

Cleo's death brought changes which Gwen is prayerfully adjusting to. Day by day, God is healing her heart and giving her courage to persevere.

Thank you, Gwen, for being who you are; a woman who loves God and others, too.

SUDDENLY, THE STARTLED COUPLE

Our local newspaper ran the story of a man and his wife whose boat had capsized in Lake Verret. They were in full view of another man who was looking out his camp window. Seeing their wild thrashing in the water, and hearing their desperate cries, he ran outside shouting, "Stand up, stand up!!!"

The article read, "Suddenly, the startled coupled stopped struggling, stood up in the waist deep water, and walked to shore."

Stop struggling. Cry unto God. In each and every situation, be sober-minded enough to whisper a prayer. He will hear and deliver you from every fear.

In spite of what may be happening, you can maintain undisturbed composure by remaining sober-minded and prayerful.

Stand to your feet Christian, look up, and view the distant shore where Jesus waits with arms open wide.

Always remember that Jesus is praying for you.

THAT BROTHER IS SO ANNOYING

My heart was load with the "cares of the world: as I drove to the church's Tuesday night prayer meeting. Ordinarily this prayer meeting was rewarding and invigorating. Regretfully, my heart's condition prevented me from entering His gates with thanksgiving and into His courts with praise, as scriptures tells us to. **(Psalm 100:4)**

Thirsting to be in His manifested presence again, I took my station to the right of the pulpit kneeling at the altar. The comforting adorning of His presence did not descend.

"Striking a dry well" left me feeling frustrated. Looking up helplessly, I asked God to please usher me into the secret place. But it was as though the heavens were brass. As my prayers bounced off the ceiling falling back onto my shoulders, I heard a familiar sound. I didn't much care for that sound.

"Oh, no. P-l-e-e-e-z-e," I moaned, "not him." It was Brother Maxwell marching (or should I say, "stomping") through the sanctuary praying loudly while thrusting his head back and forth. The sight and sound were both annoying to me.

My instantaneous plan was to wait until he passed by, turned, and headed to the back of the church; then I would try again to approach the Lord. If I struck out one more time, I was resigned to get my purse and Bible and go onto the house. My plan was no match for God's. The instant Brother Maxwell passed by me a spark of the Holy Ghost was transferred from him to me. Wow! I was jump-started with a powerful anointing to pray and touch the heart of God.

The time following was so sweet as He graciously allowed me to linger in His presence basking in His love. My Father knew that I had understood and received His reproof; therefore He didn't scold me.

Proverbs 15:31 teaches that, "The ear that heareth the reproof of life abideth among the wise."

Thank you, God, for not leaving me to walk in my own understanding, for allowing me to hear the reproof of life, and for forgiving me more times than I can count.

THE CHRISTIAN GOLD RUSH THAT WASN'T

Calling a former church member to ask if he knew the phone number of a mutual friend wasn't something I hesitated doing. When our brief conversation ended, I knew I would hesitate before calling him again.

The change in his voice, after he gave the information I needed, was obvious. It was as though he shifted into another gear positioning himself to deliver his well- practiced sales pitch.

He quickly told of quitting his job to work fulltime selling gold to Christians. The master plan was that Christians were going to "buy up all the gold and pay off the national debt."

He continued explaining this neat and nifty plan without allowing me to get a word in edgewise. He boasted that he actually didn't have to work, because he had recruited others to work for him selling gold certificates. His income had skyrocketed, and he and his wife had both quit their jobs. He and his family were now enjoying a treasure trove of new wealth.

Well, it's been said, "I may have been born at night, but it wasn't last night!" The veneer of this Ponzi scheme was transparent. Transparent to me, that is. Our one-way conversation ended as quickly as it had started.

I thought about this man several times in the months following and wondered how his kingdom building plan had panned out. Someone who knew him well said that he had been rehired at his old job and that he was also working the nightshift at Applebee's Grill and Bar washing dishes. His wife's still-new Lexis sat in their driveway while she sought employment. I was told years later that he was still working the two jobs to help alleviate their debt burden.

Before being enticed by the gold buying greed-orientated error, he and his family had a comfortable manner of living. They lived in an attractive two-story brick home in a cozy country setting with their two daughters. However, the extra income provided by his wife working part-time coupled with his being fully employed had not been enough to scratch their itch for more.

The Apostle Paul warned young Timothy with these words:
❖ **1st Timothy 6:6-10** But godliness with contentment is great gain; for we brought nothing into this world, and it is certain we can carry nothing out. And having food and raiment let us be therewith content. But they that will be (desire to be) rich fall into temptation and a snare, and into many foolish and hurtful lusts, which drown men in destruction and perdition. For the love of money is the root of all evil, which, while some coveted after, and pierced themselves through with many sorrows.

❖ **Job 22:21,24** ... Acquaint now thyself with Him, and be at peace; thereby good shall come unto thee. Then shalt thou lay up gold as dust...

There may not be more eloquent words to adequately describe the benefits of being acquainted with God.

The words, "lay up gold as dust" reminds me that the only way to collect dust is to be still. You just can't collect dust while moving in a frenzy.

We "acquaint ourselves with Him" by sitting at His feet listening and learning. It is then that we are encased with the incorruptible gold dust that comes from God alone.
Jesus strongly rebuked the last-day Laodicean church for being consumed with worldly pursuits. In Revelation 3:18 He adds, "I counsel thee to buy of me gold tried in the fire, that thou mayest be rich..."

Yes, God desires that His people be rich. Rich toward Him in precious faith and love, rich in an abundance of good works, and enriched by the indwelling Spirit of our Risen Lord.

1st John 2:15-16 clearly instructs believers to, "Love not the world, neither the things that are in the world. If any man love the world, the love of the Father is not in him."

UPDATE: The 73-year-old former Tennessee lawmaker who led the multimillion-dollar Ponzi scheme, Larry Bates, was sentenced to more than 21 years behind bars. Bates and three of his relatives were found guilty in May 2017 of mail and wire fraud. Prosecutors said the defendants keep $87 million for their personal use.

THE CLOSEST ONE TO ETERNITY
WITHOUT YOU

It was an unusual prayer that I had not prayed before and have not prayed since. It had to have been the Lord, because it certainly wasn't me.

When in the church's prayer room before the Sunday evening service, with head bowed and eyes closed, I prayed, "Lord, show me the one closest to eternity without you." There before my eyes was the blackest black imaginable. It looked like an immense black velvet-like bottomless tunnel as it spiraled downward. I felt as though I had plunged into the black emptiness. My instinctive reaction was to pull my shoulders back as if resisting a strong g-force. As my free-fall accelerated, I began earnestly, fearfully, praying frantic prayers for mercy. My loud tearful praying was overheard by others, but, remarkably, no one interfered. To this day, the shear panic that gripped my soul remains a vivid memory.

As quickly as the scene had appeared, it disappeared leaving me exhausted. I didn't speak to anyone before going in the sanctuary and taking a seat for the evening service. The minister gave an altar call at the conclusion of his message. I immediately noticed a woman at the altar whom I had not seen before. She was about forty years old, with dark hair, and a small-medium frame. She prayed alone quietly. I felt drawn to her as I approached the altar and stood behind her praying silently. She seemed resigned. Though there was no outward show of illness or of anything amiss, I knew that she was "the one closest to eternity without God." The peace of God was there ministering to her deepest need. I stayed until she stood, turned around, and returned to her seat. We did not speak. Neither had she known that I was there.

Ten days later at the regular Wednesday night's service, it was announced that the woman seen at the altar praying had died. Her name was not given. She had been noticed because most everyone knew the members, and she had not been seen there before.

Yes, it's true that neither Jesus nor His disciples were known to give what modern-day churches call an "altar call." And, it's equally true that meeting Jesus at an altar, pouring out our hearts to Him, and walking away with the "peace that passes understanding" is a soul-cleansing life-changing unforgettable experience.

The altar call that the unnamed woman responded to may have been her first and it may have been her last. She met Him there. He met her there, but not without going before and meeting her need in the prayer room.

It was there in the prayer room that God conquered the fear that had gripped her soul and released her to yield fully to Him.

THE HEARTBREAK OF ALGEBRA

You may recall an ointment ad which talked about the "heartbreak of psoriasis." Actually, I have never suffered from the "heartbreak of psoriasis," but I have watched my daughter suffer through the "heartbreak of Algebra."

Talk about a mental glitch! For my daughter, Susie, high school Algebra was just that. It seemed that no amount of coaching could get the basics across to her. Even after school tutoring didn't work. Finally, we heard about a summer tutoring program offered at Louisiana State University Laboratory School.

The admission assessment showed her comprehension to be only a seven on a scale from one to fifteen. She began the course very discouraged but worked hard and completed all of the assignments. At the end of it, she was re-evaluated and found her score at level twelve. When we talked about it, her feathers were all fallen for sure. I encouraged her by explaining that what was important was not the level of comprehension but the distance of increase. She had increased five points from where she had begun, which was remarkable.

Today, the struggling Algebra student has become a wife, mother of three, and a schoolteacher. Her former tutors had no way of knowing what she was to become.

Let's relate this experience to peoples' walks in God. If someone is said to be on a level seven in comprehending the things of God, when others feel they should be on level fifty, they err not being in a position to see the depth of darkness He has brought them from or where He intends to bring them. They, like all of us, are on a never ending journey.

When the Apostle Paul told the chief captain that he was a Roman citizen, **(Acts 22:28)** "... the captain answered, with a great sum obtained I this freedom. And Paul said, But I was free born," meaning his father was a Roman citizen.

Perhaps you were "free born" in the sense that you were born into a God-fearing church family, that your youth was spent in church and in going to church camps. Maybe you were born being exposed to the love of the truth. I hope so. But this doesn't entitle you to judge someone who was born into darkness. You may be judging (condemning) a person whom God has brought a long way. We are not in a position to see their struggles in comprehension or their determination to grow in God. A haughty religious spirit can be brought to the foot of the Cross where there is room for all.

Matthew 7:2 For with what judgment ye judge, ye shall be judged: and with what measure ye measure, it shall be measured to you again.

THE TURNING POINT FOR JUDAS ISCARIOT

The turning point for Judas Iscariot occurred when Mary of Bethany poured a pound of expensive spikenard ointment on the feet of Jesus in preparation for His burial.

John 12:6 records that he objected because, "he was a thief, and had the bag, and bore what was in it." He wasn't alone in unfavorably reacting to Mary's generous and appropriate act though. Judas' sentiment was also the objection of others standing near including some of the disciples.

Mary's act of love and devotion tipped the scales in the heart of Judas. He then left the sacrificial Lamb of God, went unto the chief priests, and asked, "What will ye give me, and I will deliver him unto you? **(Matthew 26:15)** He bargained with them for thirty pieces of silver, just as was foretold in **Zechariah 11:13**.

Judas did not profit from the blood money. Again, just as scripture had foretold, He threw the silver pieces down in the temple, after he repented that he had betrayed innocent blood. He then proceeded to kill himself. Judas never recognized that the innocent blood he betrayed belonged to the Lamb of God. **(Matthew 27:3)**

- ❖ **Mark 8:36-37** For what shall it profit a man, if he shall gain the whole world, and lose his own soul? Or what shall a man give in exchange for his soul?

THEN THERE AROSE A REASONING

Luke 9:44-46 Let these sayings sink down into your ears; for the Son of man shall be delivered into the hands of men. But they understood not this saying, and it was hidden from them, that they perceived it not; and they feared to ask him of that saying. <u>Then there arose a reasoning</u> among them, which of them should be the greatest.

This is the only recorded occasion where Jesus used the expression, "sink down into your ears." You would think that whatever would "sink down into your ears" would end up in your heart, but this was not the case. Notice that "they understood not this saying" and that "<u>then</u> there arose a reasoning."

Twelve New Testament scriptures say, "reasoned among themselves," and four others say, "reasoning among themselves." All of these "reasonings" of man led to disputes and erroneous conclusions.

When we do not understand direction from the Lord and begin to "reason among ourselves," trouble and sorrow are just ahead.

His word promises us in:
Proverbs 28:5 ...they that seek the Lord understand all things.

You may not understand aerospace dynamics. However, He will impart the understanding you need day-by-day to be the overcomer He needs you to be. ☺

The disciples could not have been further off the mark than to quarrel over "which of them should be the greatest," when He was trying to prepare them for what was to come. Notice, too, 'They were afraid to ask him." Because they were afraid to ask, they became perplexed as they leaned on their own understanding.

Later, as Jesus walked toward His appointment in Jerusalem, **Mark 10:32**, recorded the emotions of His disciples by revealing, "... as they followed, they were afraid."

We, too, may at times, be afraid when following Jesus in what is to us uncharted territory. Put your hand in His and take each step one day at a time. As you are coursing through the unknown zones of your life, remember that whatever you focus on will be magnified.

Keep your focus on Him as you rejoice in the words of King David:
   Psalm 69:30 I will praise the name of God with a song, and will magnify him with thanksgiving.

The wisdom found in Proverbs instructs us to:
   Proverbs 3:5-6 Trust in the Lord with all thine heart, and <u>lean not unto thine own understanding</u>. In all thy ways acknowledge him, and he shall direct your paths.

THEY WON'T LET ME IN

The bride-to-be insisted that I promise to attend her wedding. I agreed not wanting to offend her or to appear that her big day was not important to me. The absolute truth was that it wasn't important to me and, to this day, I am surprised that I made the forty-four mile round trip drive by myself.

The Town of Greensburg is a centerpiece of small town charm. The surrounding dairy farms and agriculture provide its income base. Greensburg's residence live lives similar to what their ancestors lived.

Finding the church was no problem since it was located directly in the middle of town. I was thinking how picturesque the setting was. The church had a neat, clean, and well-kept appearance with a coiffured lawn.

I felt a little uneasy being there by myself, but nonetheless, I walked in and took a seat midway down the aisle on the bride's side. There was a pleasant aroma coming from the well-worn wooden pews that were now crowded with well-wishers. It wasn't long before I sensed something was wrong. I glanced in both directions wondering why the atmosphere had become surreal. The people appeared to be lifeless mannequins. I gasped at the realization that a toxic plume had shrouded these people in complacency. "Oh, but wait a minute," I thought, "there is a beautiful Cross above the baptistery and each pew has a supply of tattered hymnals." But it was all too apparent that these items of "outward show" had not brought life within.

By now, the bride and groom had both made their way down the center aisle and the minister had begun the vows. The bride's father seated on the front row averted my attention. The noisy baby that he was jostling on his lap had captivated this father so much that he wasn't concerned about what was happening at the altar.

With heartfelt grief, my eyes again panned the bizarre phenomenon. I bowed my head and prayed asking, "What's wrong here, Lord?" Looking up, I saw Jesus standing outside the church window looking in. He didn't appear as the conquering Lion of the tribe of Judah or as the King of Kings. His face was ashen. His head was bowed. His chest looked as though it was caved in. He was in intense pain. My spirit shrieked, "JESUS, what's the matter?" He then spoke in a voice too poignant for words to describe. Hanging His head, He moaned, "They won't let me in."

I fervently prayed in silence, "Yes, You can come in. You can come in my heart!" I then prayed that Jesus would somehow come into that church through the couple at the altar.

My friend, what do the scriptures mean when they say:
  Romans 8:9 Now if any man have not the Spirit of Christ, he is none of his. **:11** But if the Spirit of him that raised up Jesus from the dead dwell in you, he that raised up Christ from the dead shall also quicken your mortal bodies by His Spirit that dwelleth in you.

How can someone be His, be called by His name, and attend a church with all the tapestry of Christendom and yet, not have the Spirit that raised Him from the dead?

THIS ONE IS MINE

She wasn't meant for this world. Her stay here was short, lasting only six years. During her brief life, God used her as His instrument to produce a rich depth of love and dedication in those who allowed Him to do so. Truly, His ways are high above and past finding out.

Laura Schilling was born with a malformed heart that was unable to adequately supply her body's need. Her mother introduced Laura to her two brothers as God's special gift. Her father's heart was not so welcoming. He divorced his wife and moved to a faraway state bordering Canada. His absence necessitated that Laura, together with her mother and brothers, move into the home of her grandparents. And these were <u>grand-parents</u> indeed.

They gladly made all the necessary accommodations for Laura and her family. Their lives revolved around God, church, Laura with her special needs, and binding together as a loving family unit. It was a beautiful testimony shown to all who knew them.

The more Laura grew the less her weak heart could function. Seeing the family in church, I would wonder at this special child with the corn silk hair, large blue eyes, and translucent skin with large blue veins showing through.
I was drawn to her and hoped I could steal a closer look without being observed. God provided an optimum moment during a church service when I realized I was sitting directly behind Laura's mother who had draped her over the front of her own body like a coat that had been put

on backwards. Laura's lanky limbs hung dangling uselessly. It was a heartrending sight that was quickly eased by the peaceful calm emitted by her mother.

When we stood with the congregation to worship, I found myself looking almost directly into Laura's face, which was still resting on her mother's shoulder. I smiled realizing I had been given a special moment to privately gaze upon His precious gift. At that instant the Lord spoke and told me something I had already concluded. He shared, "This one is mine." As quick as an echo, I agreed and said, "Oh, I know it!"

Laura Schilling was not a mistake. The Creator accomplished through her short six-year life just what He had intended. She was His instrument used to carve in the hearts of those who loved her an awareness and appreciation of Him that they otherwise may not have obtained. Laura completed her mission and met her Creator face to face on Sunday December 4, 1983. And I know she was not disappointed and had no complaints. After all, she was fearfully and wonderfully made!

WELCOME TO SONIC, MAY I TAKE YOUR ORDER?

As a fatherless teenager working a before and after school job at Sonic Drive-In, Roy Wilson knew how important his job income was to his mother and to him. But that wasn't the only reason he tolerated the manager's verbal abuse.

Roy's other reason and perhaps the most significant one to him was that as a young Christian, he did not want to offend anyone, even an abusive person. Roy had been taught in church youth camp that conducting his life so as not to reproach the name of Christ was of utmost importance. Roy didn't want to disappoint his Savior.

However, working at Sonic with a combative must-have-control manager who knew how to push his buttons presented a challenge Roy was not prepared to handle. He endured verbal insults, unreasonable work demands, and erratic work schedules that were intended to entice him into his manager's lust for confrontation and conquest. Roy knew he was being tempted to take matters into his own hands, and he was determined to avoid stepping into that snare.

When Roy's anger tipped his endurance scale, he cried, "God you <u>must</u> help me! I cannot take this anymore!" On and on he prayed and sobbed into the night dreading to face yet another morning at Sonic.

The next morning, still feeling the burden of dread, he rode his bicycle to Sonic expecting to take his assigned position at the order taking microphone. His eyes did a double take when he noticed the seldom-seen Sonic owner manning the order taking microphone himself instead. The morning rush was on. The manager's absence was evident but there was no time to question it. Roy quickly began helping with preparations while hearing the owner repeatedly say, "Welcome to Sonic, may I take your order?"

As the time neared for Roy to leave for school, the owner spoke to him in a fatherly tone, "Son, I've heard reports of how mistreated you've been here. You have done your work well. I have taken care of this situation. There will be a new manager here when you return this afternoon."

Roy was astonished at the owner's words and actions. He fully understood that God had come through for him. He also learned that he should have called upon God long before exceeding his endurance limit.

The following Sunday Roy smiled from deep within when his pastor quoted these scriptures:
Exodus 14:13-14 Fear not, stand still, and see the salvation of the Lord which he will show you today; for the Egyptians whom ye have seen today, ye shall see them again no more forever. The Lord shall fight for you, and ye shall hold your peace.

WELL, HE WON'T BE HERE TOMORROW NIGHT!

Asa Ewing was hard to be persuaded. He and his wife, Ida, were staunch believers in the denomination they attended while raising a large family. Asa was well-known and well-liked in the community even though he had his own way of looking at things.

His grandson, Mike, tells of the time that he was riding with him in his truck on the Jonesville Highway. They were a little past Seven Oaks Grocery when they passed an old man walking on the roadside.

Asa spoke (some might say, "acknowledged") the old man by waving his hand. The man kept walking without returning a wave. This was entirely unacceptable to Asa, who then drove down to the Patton Road and turned around heading back the way he came. He stopped his truck as it came alongside the old man and yelled to him, "Say, fella, you didn't wave to me when I drove by! I'm going down to Seven Oaks Grocery and turn around. When you see me coming, you'd better speak to me."

Mike reported that they saw the old man standing still and straining to see as far as he could. As soon as Asa's truck came into full view, he started waving both hands back and forth over his head. And he waved, and he waved, and he waved until Asa's truck was out of sight.

For Asa, nothing was complicated. It was either right or it was wrong, and he wanted everything to be right. He resisted when first told of the wonderful baptism in the Holy Ghost by his cousin, Lettie Belle Ford, who had received this marvelous gift at a Sandy Lake brush harbor revival. She continued to invite Asa and his wife to church though they weren't inclined to go.

After many invitations, Ida relented and went. The word of God was preached in a powerful way, she yielded her heart to God, and He filled her with the Holy Ghost.

After seeing the change in Ida, he became curious enough to attend a church service. The powerful worship service refreshed the congregation but left Asa wondering what he had gotten himself into.

As the preacher approached the podium, he felt the Spirit had lifted, and he knew the reason why. He bellowed, "Well, I see the old devil has come to church tonight." To which Asa responded, "Well, he won't be here tomorrow night!"

Fortunately for Asa, God used his desire to have things done right. God was to use that desire to draw him into the love of the truth. The drawing power of the Holy Ghost working with the evidence he had seen in others, persuaded Asa to go to Sandy Lake Pentecostal Church a time or two.

Then it happened. The blessing of the Holy Ghost was given to him, too. Asa Ewing became a true witness in the community delivering many souls, including his descendants, who knew him to be a man who wanted things done right.

WHAT'S EATING YOU?

It was announced that Vincent Tan, a Malaysian evangelist and former drug lord would be speaking at church the following Sunday. This was of special interest to me since my brother was then a prisoner in Malaysia. I looked forward to hearing this man's testimony.

Someone in the church office told me how to get in touch with Brother Tan. A man with a pleasant voice answered the phone and listened as I told him of my brother's miserable predicament.

Gordon had been convicted of drug trafficking and sentenced to life imprisonment, plus six strokes of the cane in this Muslim country that has no extradition policy with the United States. This made for an insurmountable situation. Insurmountable, that is, for you and me, but certainly not for God.

Brother Tan and I met the following afternoon at a ministry he was visiting. We shook hands feeling the warmth fellow believers feel even though they don't know each other.

I shared more of Gordon's unfortunate circumstance and asked that he visit him and attempt to share the gospel. He promised but made it clear that it might be some time before he was in Malaysia again.

Sunday was a long time coming, as I was eager to hear him speak. He launched into his testimony using descriptive phrases to paint a clear picture of his utter wickedness. It was shocking. He had been a major drug lord in the Golden Triangle; principally Burma, Laos, and Thailand.

His description left me blare-eyed and wondering why God extended mercy, grace, loving kindness, and eternal life to such a creature. Then I remembered that these benefits are bestowed upon us because of who He is, not because we deserve them.

He told us of his rivalry disposal operation, which guaranteed his kingpin status. He had eliminated seventeen competitors by dropping each one in an acid filled vat. It was neat and efficient. After all, homicide without a corpse is an almost perfect crime.

As he spoke, I gasped and held my right wrist with my left hand, and stammered to the Lord, "My God, I shook the hand of a man who murdered seventeen people!" I stared at my right hand expecting it to fall off. I felt my body was still there at the church service but that the rest of me had checked out. However, this man spoke with confident authority knowing who it was that was empowering him.

Surely, he had been plagued with remorse. Remorse, a noun meaning "deep and painful regret for wrongdoing," comes from the word "morsel," which means "a small portion of food or bite." To have remorse indicates the same thing is eating at you over and over. In a sense, remorse occurs when we allow the same regret to bite us over and over.

How was remorse not eating him alive as the acid had eaten his rivals? Clearly, he had taken God at His word. Who can explain the gracious forgiveness and cleansing offered to us by God through the Blood of Jesus?

Do you have lingering deep and painful regret for wrongdoing? Well, my friend, who doesn't? You probably don't have more than a man who murdered seventeen sin-laden drug dealers.

As countless other unworthy people have, confess your sin, submit to God, and allow Him to cleanse your heart, mind, and spirit continually during your earth journey.

NOTE: A year later in December 1987, a letter arrived from Brother Vincent detailing a visit he had with my brother. God was letting me know that He had given him an opportunity to be faithful to his promise.

YE WORSHIP YE KNOW NOT WHAT

Global archeological discoveries have yet to unearth a civilization or culture that did not worship. Worshiping God or gods is universal to man's history. Clearly, this is not true of other animals.

Dogs do not worship the moon, giraffes do not worship trees, and neither do lizards worship mountains. However, man's civilizations worship the moon, trees, and mountains.

According to **Ecclesiastes 3:11**, "...He hath set the world (Hebrew #5769 eternity) in their heart..." God has given man an awareness of Him, an awareness of the seasons, and of the passing of time. He has chosen not to instill this in any other of His creations.

Abram's father, Terah, was an idol worshiper who worshiped many gods. The twelfth chapter of Genesis tells of God calling Abram out of his country, out from his kinsmen, and from his father's house unto a land that He would show him.

He was called out to serve the purposes of God in revealing Himself as the One God Jehovah to a people who would be called by His name and in whose hearts He would write His law.

Joshua 24:1-27 capsulates the history of God's "called out ones" until the 14th Century B.C. He admonishes the people in verse: 14: **"**Now, therefore, fear the Lord, and serve him in sincerity and in truth; and put away the gods which your fathers served on the other side of the river...; but as for me and my house, we will serve the Lord."

Knowledge of the only true God Jehovah brings with it the responsibility of serving Him alone and forsaking all other "little g" gods.

Notice the conversation initiated by Jesus with the unnamed Samaritan woman at Jacob's well recorded in the fourth chapter of the Gospel of John. She was concerned about what was actually a non-issue. Her focus was on where to worship and not on the God who seeks true worshipers. Jesus informed her, "Ye worship ye know not what." Talk about a blunt and to-the-point answer! He told her just what she needed to know.

Notice the eight woes Jesus pronounced upon those identified as scribes, Pharisees, and hypocrites in the twenty-third chapter of the Gospel of Matthew. Among the contemptuous words He spoke are these, "Ye blind guides, who strain at a gnat, and swallow a camel." This is just one scripture example of a "religious without relationship" attitude among "religious" people.

We are given opportunity to know God personally, to understand Him by receiving His Spirit, by diligent study of His word, and by faithfulness in prayer.

If you do these things, you will undoubtedly know the God you worship.

YE HAVE NOT SPOKEN THE THING THAT IS RIGHT

How offended and disappointed is God when people who are called by His name do not speak the thing that is right about Him?

God spoke in **Job 42:7** to Eliphaz, one of "Job's helpers," and said, "My wrath is kindled against thee and thy two friends; for ye have not spoken of me the thing that is right, as my servant Job hath."

God was so disappointed in these men's failure to know and understand Him that His wrath was stirred against them. Although they evidently did not have any "written word of God," much less His indwelling Spirit, they still fell short of God's expectation. This should be a sobering reminder of our responsibility to know and understand God.

Jeremiah 9:23-24 Thus saith the Lord, Let not the wise man glory in his wisdom, neither the mighty man glory in his might, let not the rich man glory in riches but let him that glorieth glory in this, that he understandeth and knoweth me, that I am the Lord who exerciseth loving-kindness, judgment, and righteousness, in the earth; for in these things I delight, saith the Lord.

Tragically, I heard a "minister" say, in defense of his own lifestyle, "If Jesus were alive today, He would wear designer jeans." To substantiate this statement, he stated that Jesus had wealthy friends like Lazarus, Mary, and

Martha, and that before He was crucified He wore an expensive purple robe as a sign of His affluence.

But listen to what **Mark 15:17-20** has to say about this expensive purple robe:

"And they (the Roman soldiers) clothed him with purple, and plaited a crown of thorns, and put it about his head, and began to salute him, Hail, King of the Jews. And they smote him on the head with a reed, and did spit upon him, and bowing their knees, worshiped him. And when they had mocked him, they took off the purple from him, **and put his own clothes on him**, and led him out to crucify him."

Imagine the "borrowed" purple robe, which was put on Him to mock Him, being ripped off after hours of oozing blood and serum had coagulated through the fabric. This cruel act of mockery only added to His intense agony.

We are not in a position to appreciate the pain and agony He feels even today when those who are called by His name fail to love and understand Him as they should.
Those who truly know Him and love Him will learn to speak the thing that is right about Him during all their earthly trials and tribulations.

YOU ARE GOING TO GET
YOUR PURSE AND COME HOME

"You are going to get your purse and come home," were not the words Claire Watkins would have ever expected to hear from her husband. She had faithfully worked fourteen years as their church's secretary/treasurer. Claire thought she had just about heard and seen everything there was to be heard and seen. But this day she had reached an impasse.

The week prior, a woman had come to the church office and handed the pastor a four-hundred dollar free-will cash offering saying that she wanted to give it to the church. Claire had heard her words and had seen the exchange. She wondered when the pastor took the cash and put it in his pocket.

When the contributor returned days later asking to be receipted for her donation, the pastor instructed Claire to issue a Contribution Statement. To say that this instruction caused Claire to have a conflict would be incorrect. There was no conflict in her heart or mind. She could not issue a church receipt for a donation the church had not received. The only question was what she would say to the pastor.

A phone call to her husband resolved the matter. "You are going to get your purse and come home," was his firm uncompromising response. Claire's work as the church's secretary/treasurer had abruptly ended.

In the ensuing years, though they had quietly found another church, this pastor would shun both Claire and her husband at funerals and other functions. Although feeling hurt and disappointed by his actions, they guarded their hearts toward him hoping this would make a way for God to convict his heart and bring cleansing.

Jesus spoke these words while instructing His disciples:
Luke 16:11 If, therefore ye have not been faithful in the unrighteous money (mammon) who will commit to your trust the true riches?

Oh, my friend, how careful should we be to guard our hearts? This occurrence had been a test for the pastor, as well as for Claire and her husband. No one knows from day to day when such a test may come.

Proverbs 27:1 Boast not thyself of tomorrow; for thou knowest not what a day may bring forth.

The pastor, Claire, and her husband had not known what that day would bring forth.

A solemn warning is given in:
1st Corinthians 10:12: Wherefore, let him that thinketh he standeth take heed lest he fall.

YOU MAY HAVE TO STAY AT CRETE

All our assignments from the Lord are challenging. Let's consider Titus, a Gentile convert who was also Luke's brother, who was given an assignment by Paul when he "left him at Crete."

Titus was a strong individual whom Paul used in tasks requiring responsibility and good judgment. Paul left him on the Greek island of Crete to establish an orderly church. This turned out to be quite a daunting task.

Consider Paul's acknowledgment of the character of these people. In describing them, he uses such words as, "unruly, vain talkers, and deceivers."

And, if these descriptions aren't enough for Titus to have some serious second thoughts, read what Paul states in 1:12, "One of themselves, even a prophet of their own, said, The Cretans are always liars, evil beasts, lazy gluttons."

Wow! If I were going to choose, it certainly would not have been to minister to and be among "liars, evil beasts, and lazy gluttons." But we do not choose our assignments; God does, and with His calling comes the equipping.

Paul had other plans for Titus. He knew that he would not always be at Crete. Later, he would reassign him to Dalmatia (Yugoslavia).

You, too, will have other assignments. Be faithful and do your very best, even though for a season, you may be left at Crete.

Made in the USA
Columbia, SC
14 April 2019